A Traveller in Little Things

W. H. Hudson

I

HOW I FOUND MY TITLE

It is surely a rare experience for an unclassified man, past middle age, to hear himself accurately and aptly described for the first time in his life by a perfect stranger! This thing happened to me at Bristol, some time ago, in the way I am about to relate. I slept at a Commercial Hotel, and early next morning was joined in the big empty coffee-room, smelling of stale tobacco, by an intensely respectable-looking old gentleman, whose hair was of silvery whiteness, and who wore gold-rimmed spectacles and a heavy gold watch-chain with many seals attached thereto; whose linen was of the finest, and whose outer garments, including the trousers, were of the newest and blackest broadcloth. A glossier and at the same time a more venerable-looking "commercial" I had never seen in the west country, nor anywhere in the three kingdoms. He could not have improved his appearance if he had been on his way to attend the funeral of a millionaire. But with all his superior look he was quite affable, and talked fluently and instructively on a variety of themes, including trade, politics, and religion. Perceiving that he had taken me for what I was not—one of the army in which he served, but of inferior rank—I listened respectfully as became me. Finally he led the talk to the subject of agriculture, and the condition and prospects of farming in England. Here I perceived that he was on wholly unfamiliar ground, and in return for the valuable information he had given me on other and more important subjects, I proceeded to enlighten him. When I had finished stating my facts and views, he said: "I perceive that you know a great deal more about the matter than I do, and I will now tell you why you know more. You are a traveller in little things—in something very small—which takes you into the villages and hamlets, where you meet and converse with small farmers, innkeepers, labourers and their wives, with other persons who live on the land. In this way you get to hear a good deal about rent and cost of living, and what the people are able and not able to do. Now I am out of all that; I never go to a village nor see a farmer. I am a traveller in something very large. In the south and west I visit towns like Salisbury, Exeter, Bristol, Southampton; then I go to the big towns in the Midlands and the North, and to Glasgow and Edinburgh; and afterwards to Belfast and Dublin. It would simply be a waste of time for me to visit a town of less than fifty or sixty thousand inhabitants."

He then gave me some particulars concerning the large thing he travelled in; and when I had expressed all the interest and admiration the subject called for, he condescendingly invited me to tell him something about my own small line.

Now this was wrong of him; it was a distinct contravention of an unwritten law among "Commercials" that no person must be interrogated concerning the nature of his business. The big and the little man, once inside the hostel, which is their club as well, are on an equality. I did not remind my questioner of this—I merely smiled and said nothing, and he of course understood and respected my reticence. With a pleasant nod and a condescending let-us-say-no-more-about-it wave of the hand he passed on to other matters.

Notwithstanding that I was amused at his mistake, the label he had supplied me with was something to be grateful for, and I am now finding a use for it. And I think that if he, my labeller, should see this sketch by chance and recognise himself in it, he will say with his pleasant smile and wave of the hand, "Oh, that's his line! Yes, yes, I described him rightly enough, thinking it haberdashery or floral texts for cottage bedrooms, or something of that kind; I didn't imagine he was a traveller in anything quite so small as this."

II

THE OLD MAN'S DELUSION

We know that our senses are subject to decay, that from our middle years they are decaying all the time; but happily it is as if we didn't know and didn't believe. The process is too gradual to trouble us; we can only say, at fifty or sixty or seventy, that it is doubtless the case that we can't see as far or as well, or hear or smell as sharply, as we did a decade ago, but that we don't notice the difference. Lately I met an extreme case, that of a man well past seventy who did not appear to know that his senses had faded at all. He noticed that the world was not what it had been to him, as it had appeared, for example, when he was a plough-boy, the time of his life he remembered most vividly, but it was not the fault of his senses; the mirror was all right, it was the world that had grown dim. I found him at the gate where I was accustomed to go of an evening to watch the sun set over the sea of yellow corn and the high green elms beyond, which divide the cornfields from the Maidenhead Thicket. An old agricultural labourer, he had a grey face and grey hair and throat-beard; he stooped a good deal, and struck me as being very feeble and long past work. But he told me that he still did some work in the fields. The older farmers who had employed him for many years past gave him a little to do; he also had his old-age pension, and his children helped to keep him in comfort. He was quite well off, he said, compared to many. There was a subdued and sombre cheerfulness in him, and when I questioned him about his early life, he talked very freely in his slow old peasant way. He was born in a village in the Vale of Aylesbury, and began work as a ploughboy on a very big farm. He had a good master and was well fed, the food being bacon, vegetables, and homemade bread, also suet pudding three times a week. But what he remembered best was a rice pudding which came by chance in his way during his first year on the farm. There was some of the pudding left in a dish after the family had dined, and the farmer said to his wife, "Give it to the boy"; so he had it, and never tasted anything so nice in all his life. How he enjoyed that pudding! He remembered it now as if it had been yesterday, though it was sixty-five years ago.

He then went on to talk of the changes that had been going on in the world since that happy time; but the greatest change of all was in the appearance of things. He had had a hard life, and the hardest time was when he was a ploughboy and had to work so hard that he was tired to death at the end of every day; yet at four o'clock in the morning he was ready and glad to get up and go out to work all day again because everything looked so bright, and it made him happy just to look up at the sky and listen to the birds. In those days there were larks. The number of larks was wonderful; the sound of their singing filled the whole air. He didn't want any greater happiness than to hear them singing over his head. A few days ago, not more than half a mile from where we were standing, he was crossing a field when a lark got up singing near him and went singing over his head. He stopped to listen and said to himself, "Well now, that do remind me of old times!"

"For you know," he went on, "it is a rare thing to hear a lark now. What's become of all the birds I used to see I don't know. I remember there was a very pretty bird at that time called the yellow-hammer—a bird all a shining yellow, the prettiest of all the birds." He never saw nor heard that bird now, he assured me.

That was how the old man talked, and I never told him that yellow hammers could be seen and heard all day long anywhere on the common beyond the green wall of the elms, and that a lark was singing loudly high up over our heads while he was talking of the larks he had listened to sixty-five years ago in the Vale of Aylesbury, and saying that it was a rare thing to hear that bird now.

III

AS A TREE FALLS

At the Green Dragon, where I refreshed myself at noon with bread and cheese and beer, I was startlingly reminded of a simple and, I suppose, familiar psychological fact, yet one which we are never conscious of except at rare moments when by chance it is thrust upon us.

There are many Green Dragons in this world of wayside inns, even as there are many White Harts, Red Lions, Silent Women and other incredible things; but when I add that my inn is in a Wiltshire village, the headquarters of certain gentlemen who follow a form of sport which has long been practically obsolete in this country, and indeed throughout the civilised world, some of my readers will have no difficulty in identifying it.

After lunching I had an hour's pleasant conversation with the genial landlord and his buxom good-looking wife; they were both natives of a New Forest village and glad to talk about it with one who knew it intimately. During our talk I happened to use the words—I forget what about—"As a tree falls so must it lie." The landlady turned on me her dark Hampshire eyes with a sudden startled and pained look in them, and cried: "Oh, please don't say that!'

"Why not?" I asked. "It is in the Bible, and a quite common saying."

"I know," she returned, "but I can't bear it—I hate to hear it!"

She would say no more, but my curiosity was stirred, and I set about persuading her to tell me. "Ah, yes," I said, "I can guess why. It's something in your past life—a sad story of one of your family—one very much loved perhaps—who got into trouble and was refused all help from those who might have saved him."

"No," she said, "it all happened before my time—long before. I never knew her." And then presently she told me the story.

When her father was a young man he lived and worked with his father, a farmer in Hampshire and a widower. There were several brothers and sisters, and one of the sisters, named Eunice, was most loved by all of them and was her father's favourite on account of her beauty and sweet disposition. Unfortunately she became engaged to a young man who was not liked by the father, and when she refused to break her engagement to please him he was dreadfully angry and told her that if she went against him and threw herself away on that worthless fellow he would forbid her the house and would never see or speak to her again.

Being of an affectionate disposition and fond of her father it grieved her sorely to disobey him, but her love compelled her, and by-and-by she went away and was married in a neighbouring village where her lover had his home. It was not a happy marriage, and after a few anxious years she fell into a wasting illness, and when it became known to her that she was near her end she sent a message by a brother to the old father to come and see her before she died. She had never ceased to love him, and her one insistent desire was to receive his forgiveness and blessing before finishing her life. His answer was, "As a tree falls so shall it lie." He would not go near her. Shortly afterwards the unhappy young wife passed away.

The landlady added that the brother who had taken the message was her father, that he was now eighty-two years old and still spoke of his long dead and greatly loved sister, and always said he had never forgiven and would never forgive his father, dead half a century ago, for having refused to go to his dying daughter and for speaking those cruel words.

IV

"BLOOD"

A STORY OF TWO BROTHERS

A certain titled lady, great in the social world, was walking down the village street between two ladies of the village, and their conversation was about some person known to the two who had behaved in the noblest manner in difficult circumstances, and the talk ran on between the two like a duet, the great lady mostly silent and paying but little attention to it. At length the subject was exhausted, and as a proper conclusion to round the discourse off, one of them remarked: "It is what I have always said,—there's nothing like blood!" Whereupon the great person returned, "I don't agree with you: it strikes me you two are always praising blood, and I think it perfectly horrid. The very sight of a black pudding for instance turns me sick and makes me want to be a vegetarian."

The others smiled and laboriously explained that they were not praising blood as an article of diet, but had used the word in its other and partly metamorphical sense. They simply meant that as a rule persons of good blood or of old families had better qualities and a higher standard of conduct and action than others.

The other listened and said nothing, for although of good blood herself she was an out-and-out democrat, a burning Radical, burning bright in the forests of the night of dark old England, and she considered that all these lofty notions about old families and higher standards were confined to those who knew little or nothing about the life of the upper classes.

She, the aristocrat, was wrong, and the two village ladies, members of the middle class, were right, although they were without a sense of humour and did not know that their distinguished friend was poking a little fun at them when she spoke about black puddings.

They were right, and it was never necessary for Herbert Spencer to tell us that the world is right in looking for nobler motives and ideals, a higher standard of conduct, better, sweeter manners, from those who are highly placed than from the ruck of men; and as this higher, better life, which is only possible in the leisured classes, is correlated with the "aspects which please," the regular features and personal beauty, the conclusion is the beauty and goodness or "inward perfections" are correlated.

All this is common, universal knowledge: to all men of all races and in all parts of the world it comes as a shock to hear that a person of a noble countenance has been guilty of an ignoble action. It is only the ugly (and bad) who fondly cherish the delusion that beauty doesn't matter, that it is only skin-deep and the rest of it.

Here now arises a curious question, the subject of this little paper. When a good old family, of good character, falls on evil days and is eventually submerged in the classes beneath, we know that the aspects which please, the good features and expression, will often persist for long generations. Now this submerging process is perpetually going on all over the land and so it has been for centuries. We notice from year to year the rise from the ranks of numberless men to the highest positions, who are our leaders and legislators, owners of great estates who found great families and receive titles. But we do not notice the corresponding decline and final disappearance of those who were highly placed, since this is a more gradual process and has nothing sensational about it. Yet the two processes are equally great and far-reaching in their effects, and are like those two of Elaboration and Degeneration which go on side by side for ever in nature, in the animal world; and like darkness and light and heat and cold in the physical world.

As a fact, the country is full of the descendants of families that have "died out." How long it takes to blot out or blur the finer features and expression we do not know, and the time probably varies according to the length of the period during which the family existed in its higher phase. The question which confronts us is: Does the higher or better nature, the "inward perfections" which are correlated with the aspects which please, endure too, or do those who fall from their own class degenerate morally to the level of the people they live and are one with?

It is a nice question. In Sussex, with Mr. M. A. Lower, who has written about the vanished or submerged families of that county, for my guide as to names, I have sought out persons of a very humble condition, some who were shepherds and agricultural labourers, and have been surprised at the good faces of many of them, the fine, even noble, features and expression, and with these an exceptionally fine character. Labourers on the lands that were once owned by their forefathers, and children of long generations of labourers, yet still exhibiting the marks of their aristocratic descent, the fine features and expression and the fine moral qualities with which they are correlated.

I will now give in illustration an old South American experience, an example, which deeply impressed me at the time, of the sharp contrast between a remote descendant of aristocrats and a child of the people in a country where class distinctions have long ceased to exist.

It happened that I went to stay at a cattle ranch for two or three months one summer, in a part of the country new to me, where I knew scarcely anyone. It was a good spot for my purpose, which was bird study, and this wholly occupied my mind. By-and-by I heard about two brothers, aged respectively twenty-three and twenty-four years, who lived in the neighbourhood on a cattle ranch inherited from their father, who had died young. They had no relations and were the last of their name in that part of the country, and their grazing land was but a remnant of the estate as it had been a century before. The name of the brothers first attracted my attention, for it was that of an old highly-distinguished family of Spain, two or three of whose adventurous sons had gone to South America early in the seventeenth century to seek their fortunes, and had settled there. The real name need not be stated: I will call it de la Rosa, which will serve as well as another. Knowing something of the ancient history of the family I became curious to meet the brothers, just to see what sort of men they were who had blue blood and yet lived, as their forbears had done for generations, in the rough primitive manner of the gauchos—the cattle-tending horsemen of the pampas. A little later I met the younger brother at a house in the village a few miles from the ranch I was staying at. His name was Cyril; the elder was Ambrose. He was certainly a very fine fellow in appearance, tall and strongly built, with a high colour on his open genial countenance and a smile always playing about the corners of his rather large sensual mouth and in his greenish-hazel eyes; but of the noble ancestry there was no faintest trace. His features were those of the unameliorated peasant, as he may be seen in any European country, and in this country, in Ireland particularly, but with us he is not so common. It would seem that in England there is a larger mixture of better blood, or that the improvements in features due to improved conditions, physical and moral, have gone further. At all events, one may look at a crowd anywhere in England and see only a face here and there of the unmodified plebeian type. In a very large majority the forehead will be less low and narrow, the nose less coarse with less wide-spreading alae, the depression in the bridge not so deep, the mouth not so large nor the jowl so heavy. These marks of the unimproved adult are present in all infants at birth. Lady Clara Vere de Vere's little bantling is in a sense not hers at all but the child of some ugly antique race; of a Palaeolithic mother, let us say, who lived before the last Glacial epoch and was not very much better-looking herself than an orang-utan. It is only when the bony and cartilaginous framework, with the muscular covering of the face, becomes modified, and the wrinkled brown visage of the ancient pigmy grows white and smooth, that it can be recognised as Lady Clara's own offspring. The infant is ugly, and where the infantile features survive in the adult the man is and must be ugly too, *unless the expression is good*. Thus, we may know numbers of persons who would certainly be ugly but for the redeeming expression; and this good expression, which is "feature in the making," is, like good features, an "outward sign of inward perfections."

To continue with the description of my young gentleman of blue blood and plebeian countenance, his expression not only saved him from ugliness but made him singularly attractive, it revealed a good nature, friendliness, love of his fellows, sincerity, and other pleasing qualities. After meeting and conversing with him I was not surprised to hear that he was universally liked, but regarding him critically I could not say that his manner was perfect. He was too self-conscious, too anxious to shine, too vain of his personal appearance, of his wit, his rich dress, his position as a de la Rosa and a landowner. There was even a vulgarity in him, such as one looks for in a person risen from the lower orders but does not expect in the descendant of an ancient and once lustrous family, however much decayed and impoverished, or submerged.

Shortly afterwards a gossipy old native estanciero, who lived close by, while sitting in our kitchen sipping maté, began talking freely about his neighbour's lives and characters, and I told him I had felt interested in the brothers de la Rosa; partly on account of the great affection these two had for one another, which was like an ideal friendship; and in part too on account of the ancient history of the family they came from. I had met one of them, I told him,—Cyril—a very fine fellow, but in some respects he was not exactly like my preconceived idea of a de la Rosa.

"No, and he isn't one!" shouted the old fellow, with a great laugh; and more than delighted at having a subject presented to him and at his capture of a fresh listener, he proceeded to give me an intimate history of the brothers.

The father, who was a fine and a lovable man, married early, and his young wife died in giving birth to their only child—Ambrose. He did not marry again: he was exceedingly fond of his child and was both father and mother to it and kept it with him until the boy was about nine years old, and then determined to send him to Buenos Ayres to give him a year's schooling. He himself had been taught to read as a small boy, also to write a letter, but he did not think himself equal to teach the boy, and so for a time they would have to be separated.

Meanwhile the boy had picked up with Cyril, a little waif in rags, the bastard child of a woman who had gone away and left him in infancy to the mercy of others. He had been reared in the hovel of a poor gaucho on the de la Rosa land, but the poor orphan, although the dirtiest, raggedest, most mischievous little beggar in the land, was an attractive child, intelligent, full of fun, and of an adventurous spirit. Half his days were spent miles from home, wading through the vast reedy and rushy marshes in the neighbourhood, hunting for birds' nests. Little Ambrose, with no child companion at home, where his life had been made too soft for him, was exceedingly happy with his wild companion, and they were often absent together in the marshes for a whole day, to the great anxiety of the father. But he could not separate them, because he could not endure to see the misery of his boy when they were forcibly kept apart. Nor could he forbid his child from heaping gifts in food and clothes and toys or whatever he had, on his little playmate. Nor did the trouble cease when the time came now for the boy to be sent from home to learn his letters: his grief at the prospect of being separated from his companion was too much for the father, and he eventually sent them together to the city, where they spent a year or two and came back as devoted to one another as when they went away. From that time Cyril lived with them, and eventually de la Rosa adopted him, and to make his son happy he left all he possessed to be equally divided at his death between them. He was in bad health, and died when Ambrose was fifteen and Cyril fourteen; from that time they were their own masters and refused to have any division of their inheritance but continued to live together; and had so continued for upwards of ten years.

Shortly after hearing this history I met the brothers together at a house in the village, and a greater contrast between two men it would be impossible to imagine. They were alike only in both being big, well-shaped, handsome, and well-dressed men, but in their faces they had the stamp of widely separated classes, and differed as much as if they had belonged to distinct species. Cyril, with a coarse, high-coloured skin and the primitive features I have described; Ambrose, with a pale dark skin of a silky texture, an oval face and classic features—forehead, nose, mouth and chin, and his ears small and lying against his head, not sticking out like handles as in his brother; he had black hair and grey eyes. It was the face of an aristocrat, of a man of blue blood, or of good blood, of an ancient family; and in his manner too he was a perfect contrast to his brother and friend. There was no trace of vulgarity in him; he was not self-conscious, not anxious to shine; he was modesty itself, and in his speech and manner and appearance he was, to put it all in one word, a gentleman.

Seeing them together I was more amazed than ever at the fact of their extraordinary affection for each other, their perfect amity which had lasted so many years without a rift, which nothing could break, as people said, except a woman.

But the woman who would break or shatter it had not yet appeared on the horizon, nor do I know whether she ever appeared or not, since after leaving the neighbourhood I heard no more of the brothers de la Rosa.

V

A STORY OF LONG DESCENT

It was rudely borne in upon me that there was another side to the shield. I was too much immersed in my own thoughts to note the peculiar character of the small remote old-world town I came to in the afternoon; next day was Sunday, and on my way to the church to attend morning service, it struck me as one of the oldest-looking of the small old towns I had stumbled upon in my rambles in this ancient land. There was the wide vacant space where doubtless meetings had taken place for a thousand years, and the steep narrow crooked medieval streets, and here and there some stately building rising like a castle above the humble cottage houses clustering round it as if for protection. Best of all was the church with its noble tower where a peal of big bells were just now flooding the whole place with their glorious noise.

It was even better when, inside, I rose from my knees and looked about me, to find myself in an ideal interior, the kind I love best; rich in metal and glass and old carved wood, the ornaments which the good Methody would scornfully put in the hay and stubble category, but which owing to long use and associations have acquired for others a symbolic and spiritual significance. The beauty and richness were all the fresher for the dimness, and the light was dim because it filtered through old oxydised stained glass of that unparalleled loveliness of colour which time alone can impart. It was, excepting in vastness, like a cathedral interior, and in some ways better than even the best of these great fanes, wonderful as they are. Here, recalling them, one could venture to criticise and name their several deficits:—a Wells divided, a ponderous Ely, a vacant and cold Canterbury, a too light and airy Salisbury, and so on even to Exeter, supreme in beauty, spoilt by a monstrous organ in the wrong place. That wood and metal giant, standing as a stone bridge to mock the eyes' efforts to dodge past it and have sight of the exquisite choir beyond, and of an east window through which the humble worshipper in the nave might hope, in some rare mystical moment, to catch a glimpse of the far Heavenly country beyond.

I also noticed when looking round that it was an interior rich in memorials to the long dead—old brasses and stone tablets on the walls, and some large monuments. By chance the most imposing of the tombs was so near my seat that with little difficulty I succeeded in reading and committing to memory the whole contents of the very long inscription cut in deep letters on the hard white stone. It was to the memory of Sir Ranulph Damarell, who died in 1531, and was the head of a family long settled in those parts, lord of the manor and many other things. On more than one occasion he raised a troop from his own people and commanded it himself, fighting for his king and country both in and out of England. He was, moreover, a friend of the king and his counsellor, and universally esteemed for his virtues and valour; greatly loved by all his people, especially by the poor and suffering, on account of his generosity and kindness of heart.

A very glorious record, and by-and-by I believed every word of it. For after reading the inscription I began to examine the effigy in marble of the man himself which surmounted the tomb. He was lying extended full length, six feet and five inches, his head on a low pillow, his right hand grasping the handle of his drawn sword. The more I looked at it, both during and after the service, the more convinced I became that this was no mere conventional figure made by some lapidary long after the subject's death, but was the work of an inspired artist, an exact portrait of the man, even to his stature, and that he had succeeded in giving to the countenance the very expression of the living Sir Ranulph. And what it expressed was power and authority and, with it, spirituality. A noble countenance with a fine forehead and nose, the lower part of the face covered with the beard, and long hair that fell to the shoulders.

It produced a feeling such as I have whenever I stand before a certain sixteenth-century portrait in the National Gallery: a sense or an illusion of being in the presence of a living person with whom I am engaged in a wordless conversation, and who is revealing his inmost soul to me. And it is only the work of a genius that can affect you in that way.

Quitting the church I remembered with satisfaction that my hostess at the quiet home-like family hotel where I had put up, was an educated intelligent woman (good-looking, too), and that she would no doubt be able to tell me something of the old history of the town and particularly of Sir Ranulph. For this marble man, this knight of ancient days, had taken possession of me and I could think of nothing else.

At luncheon we met as in a private house at our table with our nice hostess at the head, and beside her three or four guests staying in the house; a few day visitors to the town came in and joined us. Next to me I had a young New Zealand officer whose story I had heard with painful interest the previous evening. Like so many of the New Zealanders I had met before, he was a splendid young fellow; but he had been terribly gassed at the front and had been told by the doctors that he would not be fit to go back even if the war lasted another year, and we were then well through the third. The way the poison in his lungs affected him was curious. He had his bad periods when for a fortnight or so he would lie in his hospital suffering much and terribly depressed, and at such time black spots would appear all over his chest and neck and arms so that he would be spotted like a pard. Then the spots would fade and he would rise apparently well, and being of an energetic disposition, was allowed to do local war work.

On the other side of the table facing us sat a lady and gentleman who had come in together for luncheon. A slim lady of about thirty, with a well-shaped but colourless face and very bright intelligent eyes. She was a lively talker, but her companion, a short fat man with a round apple face and cheeks of an intensely red colour and a black moustache, was reticent, and when addressed directly replied in monosyllables. He gave his undivided attention to the thing on his plate.

The young officer talked to me of his country, describing with enthusiasm his own district which he averred contained the finest mountain and forest scenery in New Zealand. The lady sitting opposite began to listen and soon cut in to say she knew it all well, and agreed in all he said in praise of the scenery. She had spent weeks of delight among those great forests and mountains. Was she then his country-woman? he asked. Oh, no, she was English but had travelled extensively and knew a great deal of New Zealand. And after exhausting this subject the conversation, which had become general, drifted into others, and presently we were all comparing notes about our experience of the late great frost. Here I had my say about what had happened in the village I had been staying in. The prolonged frost, I said, had killed all or most of the birds in the open country round us, but in the village itself a curious thing had happened to save the birds of the place. It was a change of feeling in the people, who are by nature or training great persecutors of birds. The sight of them dying of starvation had aroused a sentiment of compassion, and all the villagers, men, women, and children, even to the roughest bush-beating boys, started feeding them, with the result that the birds quickly became tame and spent their whole day flying from house to house, visiting every yard and perching on the window-sills. While I was speaking the gentleman opposite put down his knife and fork and gazed steadily at me with a smile on his red-apple face, and when I concluded he exploded in a half-suppressed sniggering laugh.

It annoyed me, and I remarked rather sharply that I didn't see what there was to laugh at in what I had told them. Then the lady with ready tact interposed to say she had been deeply interested in my experiences, and went on to tell what she had done to save the birds in her own place; and her companion, taking it perhaps as a snub to himself from her, picked up his knife and fork and went on with his luncheon, and never opened his mouth to speak again. Or, at all events, not till he had quite finished his meal.

By-and-by, when I found an opportunity of speaking to our hostess, I asked her who that charming lady was, and she told me she was a Miss Somebody—I forget the name—a native of the town, also that she was a great favourite there and was loved by everyone, rich and poor, and that she had been a very hard worker ever since the war began, and had inspired all the women in the place to work.

"And who," I asked, "was the fellow who brought her in to lunch—a relative or a lover?"

"Oh, no, no relation and certainly not a lover. I doubt if she would have him if he wanted her, in spite of his position."

"I don't wonder at that—a perfect clown! And who is he?"

"Oh, didn't you know! Sir Ranulph Damarell."

"Good Lord!" I gasped. "That your great man—lord of the manor and what not! He may bear the name, but I'm certain he's not a descendant of the Sir Ranulph whose monument is in your church."

"Oh, yes, he is," she replied. "I believe there has never been a break in the line from father to son since that man's day. They were all knights in the old time, but for the last two centuries or so have been baronets."

"Good Lord!" I exclaimed again. "And please tell me what is he——what does he do? What is his distinction?"

"His distinction for me," she smilingly replied, "is that he prefers my house to have his luncheon in after Sunday morning service. He knows where he can get good cooking. And as a rule he invites some friend in the town to lunch with him, so that should there be any conversation at table his guest can speak for both and leave him quite free to enjoy his food."

"And what part does he take in politics and public affairs—how does he stand among your leading men?"

Her answer was that he had never taken any part in politics—had never been or desired to be in Parliament or in the County Council, and was not even a J.P., nor had he done anything for his country during the war. Nor was he a sportsman. He was simply a country gentleman, and every morning he took a ride or walk, mainly she supposed to give him a better appetite for his luncheon. And he was a good landlord to his tenants and he was respected by everybody and no one had ever said a word against him.

There was nothing now for me to say except 'Good Lord!' so I said it once more, and that made three times.

VI

A SECOND STORY OF TWO BROTHERS

Shortly after writing the story of two brothers in the last part but one I was reminded of another strange story of two brothers in that same distant land, which I heard years ago and had forgotten. It now came back to me in a newspaper from Miami, of all places in the world, sent me by a correspondent in that town. He—Mr. J. L. Rodger—some time ago when reading an autobiographical book of mine made the discovery that we were natives of the same place in the Argentine pampas—that the homes where we respectively first saw the light stood but a couple of hours' ride on horseback apart. But we were not born on the same day and so missed meeting in our youth; then left our homes, and he, after wide wanderings, found an earthly paradise in Florida to dwell in. So that now that we have in a sense met we have the Atlantic between us. He has been contributing some recollections of the pampas to the Miami paper, and told this story of two brothers among other strange happenings. I tell it in my own way more briefly.

It begins in the early fifties and ends thirty years later in the early eighties of last century. It then found its way into the Buenos Ayres newspapers, and I heard it at the time but had utterly forgotten it until this Florida paper came into my hand.

In the fifties a Mr. Gilmour, a Scotch settler, had a sheep and cattle ranch on the pampas far south of Buenos Ayres, near the Atlantic coast. He lived there with his family, and one of the children, aged five, was a bright active little fellow and was regarded with affection by one of the hired native cattlemen, who taught the child to ride on a pony, and taught him so well that even at that tender age the boy could follow his teacher and guide at a fast gallop over the plain. One day Mr. Gilmour fell out with the man on account of some dereliction of duty, and after some hot words between them discharged him there and then. The young fellow mounted his horse and rode off vowing vengeance, and on that very day the child disappeared. The pony on which he had gone out riding came home, and as it was supposed that the little boy had been thrown or fallen off, a search was made all over the estate and continued for days without result. Eventually some of the child's clothing was found on the beach, and it was conjectured that the young native had taken the child there and drowned him and left the clothes to let the Gilmours know that he had had his revenge. But there was room for doubt, as the body was never found, and they finally came to think that the clothes had been left there to deceive them, and that as the man had been so fond of the child he had carried him off. This belief started them on a wider and longer quest; they invoked the aid of the authorities all over the province; the loss of the child was advertised and a large reward offered for his recovery and agents were employed to look for him. In this search, which continued for years, Mr. Gilmour spent a large part of his fortune, and eventually it had to be dropped; and of all the family Mrs. Gilmour alone still believed that her lost son was living, and still dreamed and hoped that she would see him again before her life ended.

One day the Gilmours entertained a traveller, a native gentleman, who, as the custom was in my time on those great vacant plains where houses were far apart, had ridden up to the gate at noon and asked for hospitality. He was a man of education, a great traveller in the land, and at table entertained them with an account of some of the strange out-of-the-world places he had visited.

Presently one of the sons of the house, a tall slim good-looking young man of about thirty, came in, and saluting the stranger took his seat at the table. Their guest started and seemed to be astonished at the sight of him, and after the conversation was resumed he continued from time to time to look with a puzzled questioning air at the young man. Mrs. Gilmour had observed this in him and, with the thought of her lost son ever in her mind, she became more and more agitated until, unable longer to contain her excitement, she burst out: "O, Señor, why do you look at my son in that way?—tell me if by chance you have not met someone in your wanderings that was like him."

Yes, he replied, he had met someone so like the young man before him that it had almost produced the illusion of his being the same person; that was why he had looked so searchingly at him.

Then in reply to their eager questions he told them that it was an old incident, that he had never spoken a word to the young man he had seen, and that he had only seen him once for a few minutes. The reason of his remembering him so well was that he had been struck by his appearance, so strangely incongruous in the circumstances, and that had made him look very sharply at him. Over two years had passed since, but it was still distinct in his memory. He had come to a small frontier settlement, a military outpost, on the extreme north-eastern border of the Republic, and had seen the garrison turn out for exercise from the fort. It was composed of the class of men one usually saw in these border forts, men of the lowest type, miztiros and mulattos most of them, criminals from the gaols condemned to serve in the frontier army for their crimes. And in the midst of the low-browed, swarthy-faced, ruffianly crew appeared the tall distinguished-looking young man with a white skin, blue eyes and light hair—an amazing contrast!

That was all he could tell them, but it was a clue, the first they had had in thirty years, and when they told the story of the lost child to their guest he was convinced that it was their son he had seen—there could be no other explanation of the extraordinary resemblance between the two young men. At the same time he warned them that the search would be a difficult and probably a disappointing one, as these frontier garrisons were frequently changed: also that many of the men deserted whenever they got the chance, and that many of them got killed, either in fight with the Indians, or among themselves over their cards, as gambling was their only recreation.

But the old hope, long dead in all of them except in the mother's heart, was alive again, and the son, whose appearance had so strongly attracted their guest's attention, at once made ready to go out on that long journey. He went by way of Buenos Ayres where he was given a passport by the War Office and a letter to the Commanding Officer to discharge the blue-eyed soldier in the event of his being found and proved to be a brother to the person in quest of him. But when he got to the end of his journey on the confines of that vast country, after travelling many weeks on horseback, it was only to hear that the men who had formed the garrison two years before, had been long ordered away to another province where they had probably been called to aid in or suppress a revolutionary outbreak, and no certain news could be had of them. He had to return alone but not to drop the search; it was but the first of three great attempts he made, and the second was the most disastrous, when in a remote Province and a lonely district he met with a serious accident which kept him confined in some poor hovel for many months, his money all spent, and with no means of communicating with his people. He got back at last; and after recruiting his health and providing himself with funds, and obtaining fresh help from the War Office, he set out on his third venture; and at the end of three years from the date of his first start, he succeeded in finding the object of his search, still serving as a common soldier in the army. That they were brothers there was no doubt in either of their minds, and together they travelled home.

And now the old father and mother had got their son back, and they told him the story of the thirty years during which they had lamented his loss, and of how at last they had succeeded in recovering him:—what had he to tell them in return? It was a disappointing story. For, to begin with, he had no recollection of his child life at home—no faintest memory of mother or father or of the day when the sudden violent change came and he was forcibly taken away. His earliest recollection was of being taken about by someone—a man who owned him, who was always at the cattle-estates where he worked, and how this man treated him kindly until he was big enough to be set to work shepherding sheep and driving cattle, and doing anything a boy could do at any place they lived in, and that his owner and master then began to be exacting and tyrannical, and treated him so badly that he eventually ran away and never saw the man again. And from that time onward he lived much the same kind of life as when with his master, constantly going about from place to place, from province to province, and finally he had for some unexplained reason been taken into the army.

That was all—the story of his thirty years of wild horseback life told in a few dry sentences! Could more have been expected! The mother had expected more and would not cease to expect it. He was her lost one found again, the child of her body who in his long absence had gotten a second nature; but it was nothing but a colour, a garment, which would wear thinner and thinner, and by-and-by reveal the old deeper ineradicable nature beneath. So she imagined, and would take him out to walk to be with him, to have him all to herself, to caress him, and they would walk, she with an arm round his neck or waist; and when she released him or whenever he could make his escape from the house, he would go off to the quarters of the hired cattlemen and converse with them. They were his people, and he was one of them in soul in spite of his blue eyes, and like one of them he could lasso or break a horse and throw a bull and put a brand on him, and kill a cow and skin it, or roast it in its hide if it was wanted so; and he could do a hundred other things, though he couldn't read a book, and I daresay he found it a very misery to sit on a chair in the company of those who read in books and spoke a language that was strange to him—the tongue he had himself spoken as a child!

VII

A THIRD STORY OF TWO BROTHERS

Stories of two brothers are common enough the world over—probably more so than stories of young men who have fallen in love with their grandmothers, and the main feature in most of them, as in the story I have just told, is in the close resemblance of the two brothers, for on that everything hinges. It is precisely the same in the one I am about to relate, one I came upon a few years ago—just how many I wish not to say, nor just where it happened except that it was in the west country; and for the real names of people and places I have substituted fictitious ones. For this too, like the last, is a true story. The reader on finishing it will perhaps blush to think it true, but apart from the moral aspect of the case it is, psychologically, a singularly interesting one.

One summer day I travelled by a public conveyance to Pollhampton, a small rustic market town several miles distant from the nearest railroad. My destination was not the town itself, but a lonely heath-grown hill five miles further on, where I wished to find something that grew and blossomed on it, and my first object on arrival was to secure a riding horse or horse and trap to carry me there. I was told at once that it was useless to look for such a thing, as it was market day and everybody was fully occupied. That it was market day I already knew very well, as the two or three main streets and wide market-place in the middle of the town were full of sheep and cows and pigs and people running about and much noise of shoutings and barking dogs. However, the strange object of the strange-looking stranger in coming to the town, interested some of the wild native boys, and they rushed about to tell it, and in less than five minutes a nice neat-looking middle-aged man stood at my elbow and said he had a good horse and trap and for seven-and-sixpence would drive me to the hill, help me there to find what I wanted, and bring me back in time to catch the conveyance. Accordingly in a few minutes we were speeding out of the town drawn by a fast-trotting horse. Fast trotters appeared to be common in these parts, and as we went along the road from time to time a small cloud of dust would become visible far ahead of us, and in two or three minutes a farmer's trap would appear and rush past on its way to market, to vanish behind us in two or three minutes more and be succeeded by another and then others. By-and-by one came past driven by two young women, one holding the reins, the other playing with the whip. They were tall, dark, with black hair, and colourless faces, aged about thirty, I imagined. As they flew by I remarked, "I would lay a sovereign to a shilling that they are twins." "You'd lose your money—there's two or three years between them," said my driver. "Do you know them—you didn't nod to them nor they to you?" I said. "I know them," he returned, "as well as I know my own face when I look at myself in a glass." On which I remarked that it was very wonderful. "'Tis only a part of the wonder, and not the biggest part," he said. "You've seen what they are like and how like they are, but if you passed a day with them in the house you'd be able to tell one from the other; but if you lived a year in the same house with their two brothers you'd never be able to tell one from the other and be sure you were right. The strangest thing is that the brothers who, like their sisters, have two or three years between them, are not a bit like their sisters; they are blue-eyed and seem a different race."

That, I said, made it more wonderful still. A curiously symmetrical family. Rather awkward for their neighbours, and people who had business relations with them.

"Yes—perhaps," he said, "but it served them very well on one occasion to be so much alike."

I began to smell a dramatic rat and begged him to tell me all about it.

He said he didn't mind telling me. Their name was Prage—Antony and Martin Prage, of Red Pit Farm, which they inherited from their father and worked together. They were very united. One day one of them, when riding six miles from home, met a girl coming along the road, and stopped his horse to talk to her. She was a poor girl that worked at a dairy farm near by, and lived with her mother, a poor old widow-woman, in a cottage in the village. She was pretty, and the young man took a liking to her and he persuaded her to come again to meet him on another day at that spot; and there were many more meetings, and they were fond of each other; but after she told him that something had happened to her he never came again. When she made enquiries she found he had given her a false name and address, and so she lost sight of him. Then her child was born, and she lived with her mother. And you must know what her life was—she and her old mother and her baby and nothing to keep them. And though she was a shy ignorant girl she made up her mind to look for him until she found him to make him pay for the child. She said he had come on his horse so often to see her that he could not be too far away, and every morning she would go off in search of him, and she spent weeks and months tramping about the country, visiting all the villages for many miles round looking for him. And one day in a small village six miles from her home she caught sight of him galloping by on his horse, and seeing a woman standing outside a cottage she ran to her and asked who that young man was who had just ridden by. The woman told her she thought it was Mr. Antony Prage of Red Pit Farm, about two miles from the village. Then the girl came home and was advised what to do. She had to do it all herself as there was no money to buy a lawyer, so she had him brought to court and told her own story, and the judge was very gentle with her and drew out all the particulars. But Mr. Prage had got a lawyer, and when the girl had finished her story he got up and put just one question to her. First he called on Antony Prage to stand up in court, then he said to her, "Do you swear that the man standing before you is the father of your child?"

And just when he put that question Antony's brother Martin, who had been sitting at the back of the court, got up, and coming forward stood at his brother's side. The girl stared at the two, standing together, too astonished to speak for some time. She looked from one to the other and at last said, "I swear it is one of them." That, the lawyer said, wasn't good enough. If she could not swear that Antony Prage, the man she had brought into court, was the guilty person, then the case fell to the ground.

My informant finished his story and I asked "Was that then the end—was nothing more done about it?" "No, nothing." "Did not the judge say it was a mean dirty trick arranged between the brothers and the lawyer?" "No, he didn't—he non-suited her and that was all." "And did not Antony Prage, or both of them, go into the witness box and swear that they were innocent of the charge?" "No, they never opened their mouths in court. When the judge told the young woman that she had failed to establish her case, they walked out smiling, and their friends came round them and they went off together." "And these brothers, I suppose, still live among you at their farm and are regarded as good respectable young men, and go to chapel on Sundays, and by-and-by will probably marry nice respectable Methodist girls, and the girls' friends will congratulate them on making such good matches."

"Oh, no doubt; one has been married some time and his wife has got a baby; the other one will be married before long."

"And what do you think about it all?"

"I've told you what happened because the facts came out in court and are known to everyone. What I think about it is what I think, and I've no call to tell that."

"Oh, very well!" I said, vexed at his noncommittal attitude. Then I looked at him, but his face revealed nothing; he was just the man with a quiet manner and low voice who had put himself at my service and engaged to drive me five miles out to a hill, help me to find what I wanted and bring me back in time to catch the conveyance to my town, all for the surprisingly moderate sum of seven-and-sixpence. But he had told me the story of the two brothers; and besides, in spite of our faces being masks, if one make them so, mind converses with mind in some way the psychologists have not yet found out, and I knew that in his heart of hearts he regarded those two respectable members of the Pollhampton community much as I did.

VIII

THE TWO WHITE HOUSES: A MEMORY

There's no connection—not the slightest—between this two and the other twos; it was nevertheless the telling of the stories of the brothers which brought back to me this ancient memory of two houses. Nor were the two houses connected in any way, except that they were both white, situated on the same road, on the same side of it; also both stood a little way back from the road in grounds beautifully shaded with old trees. It was the great southern road which leads from the city of Buenos Ayres, the Argentine capital, to the vast level cattle-country of the pampas, where I was born and bred. Naturally it was a tremendously exciting adventure to a child's mind to come from these immense open plains, where one lived in rude surroundings with the semi-barbarous gauchos for only neighbours, to a great civilised town full of people and of things strange and beautiful to see. And to touch and taste.

Thus it happened that when I, a child, with my brothers and sisters, were taken to visit the town we would become more and more excited as we approached it at the end of a long journey, which usually took us two days, at all we saw—ox-carts and carriages and men on horseback on the wide hot dusty road, and the houses and groves and gardens on either side.... It was thus that we became acquainted with the two white houses, and were attracted to them because in their whiteness and green shade they looked beautiful to us and cool and restful, and we wished we could live in them.

They were well outside of the town, the nearest being about two miles from its old south wall and fortifications, the other one a little over two miles further out. The last being the farthest out was the first one we came to on our journeys to the city; it was a somewhat singular-looking building with a verandah supported by pillars painted green, and it had a high turret. And near it was a large dovecot with a cloud of pigeons usually flying about it, and we came to calling it Dovecot House. The second house was plainer in form but was not without a peculiar distinction in its large wrought-iron front gate with white pillars on each side, and in front of each pillar a large cannon planted postwise in the earth.

This we called Cannon House, but who lived in these two houses none could tell us.

When I was old enough to ride as well as any grown-up, and my occasional visits to town were made on horseback, I once had three young men for my companions, the oldest about twenty-eight, the two not more than nineteen and twenty-one respectively. I was eagerly looking out for the first white house, and when we were coming to it I cried out, "Now we are coming to Dovecot House, let's go slow and look at it."

Without a word they all pulled up, and for some minutes we sat silently gazing at the house. Then the eldest of the three said that if he was a rich man he would buy the house and pass the rest of his life very happily in it and in the shade of its old trees.

In what, the others asked, would his happiness consist, since a rational being must have something besides a mere shelter from the storm and a tree to shade him from the sun to be happy?

He answered that after securing the house he would range the whole country in search of the most beautiful woman in it, and that when he had found and made her his wife he would spend his days and years in adoring her for her beauty and charm.

His two young companions laughed scornfully. Then one of them—the younger—said that he too if wealthy would buy the house, as he had not seen another so well suited for the life he would like to live. A life spent with books! He would send to Europe for all the books he desired to read and would fill the house with them; and he would spend his days in the house or in the shade of the trees, reading every day from morning to night undisturbed by traffic and politics and revolutions in the land, and by happenings all the world over.

He too was well laughed at; then the last of the three said he didn't care for either of their ideals. He liked wine best, and if he had great wealth he would buy the house and send to Europe—O not for books nor for a beautiful wife! but for wine—wines of all the choicest kinds in bottle and casks—and fill the cellars with it. And his choice wines would bring choice spirits to help him drink them; and then in the shade of the old trees they would have their table and sit over their wine—the merriest, wittiest, wisest, most eloquent gathering in all the land.

The others in their turn laughed at him, despising his ideal, and then we set off once more.

They had not thought to put the question to me, because I was only a boy while they were grown men; but I had listened with such intense interest to that colloquy that when I recall the scene now I can see the very expressions of their sun-burnt faces and listen to the very sound of their speech and laughter. For they were all intimately known to me and I knew they were telling openly just what their several notions of a happy life were, caring nothing for the laughter of the others. I was mightily pleased that they, too, had felt the attractions of my Dovecot House as a place where a man, whatsoever his individual taste, might find a happy abiding-place.

Time rolled on, as the slow-going old storybooks written before we were born used to say, and I still preserved the old habit of pulling up my horse on coming abreast of each one of the two houses on every journey to and from town. Then one afternoon when walking my horse past the Cannon House I saw an old man dressed in black with snow-white hair and side-whiskers in the old, old style, and an ashen grey face, standing motionless by the side of one of the guns and gazing out at the distance. His eyes were blue—the dim weary blue of a tired old man's eyes, and he appeared not to see me as I walked slowly by him within a few yards, but to be gazing at something beyond, very far away. I took him to be a resident, perhaps the owner of the house, and this was the first time I had seen any person there. So strongly did the sight of that old man impress me that I could not get his image out of my mind, and I spoke to those I knew in the city, and before long I met with one who was able to satisfy my curiosity about him. The old man I had seen, he told me, was Admiral Brown, an Englishman who many years before had taken service with the Dictator Rosas at the time when Rosas was at war with the neighbouring Republic of Uruguay, and had laid siege to the city of Montevideo. Garibaldi, who was spending the years of his exile from Italy in South America, fighting as usual wherever there was any fighting to be had, flew to the help of Uruguay, and having acquired great fame as a sea-fighter was placed in command of the naval forces, such as they were, of the little Republic. But Brown was a better fighter, and he soon captured and destroyed his enemies' ships, Garibaldi himself escaping shortly afterwards to come back to the old world to renew the old fight against Austria.

When old Admiral Brown retired he built this house, or had it given to him by Rosas who, I was told, had a great affection for him, and he then had the two cannons he had taken from one of the captured ships planted at his front gate.

Shortly after that one glimpse I had had of the old Admiral, he died. And I think that when I saw him standing at his gate gazing past me at the distance, he was looking out for an expected messenger—a figure in black moving swiftly towards him with a drawn sword in his hand.

Oddly enough it was but a short time after seeing the old man at his gate that I had my first sight of an inmate of Dovecot House. While slowly riding by it I saw a lady come out from the front door—young, good-looking, very pale and dressed in the deepest mourning. She had a bowl in her hand, and going a little distance from the house she called the pigeons and down they flew in a crowd to her feet to be fed.

A few months later when passing I saw this same lady once more, and on this occasion she was coming to the gate as I rode by, and I saw her closely, for she turned and looked at me, not unseeingly like the old man, and her face was perfectly colourless and her large dark eyes the most sorrowful I had ever seen.

That was my last sight of her, nor did I see any human creature about the house after that for about two years. Then one hot summer day I caught sight of three persons who looked like servants or caretakers, sitting in the shade some distance from the house and drinking maté, the tea of the country.

Here, thought I, is an opportunity not to be lost—one long waited for! Leaving my horse at the gate I went to them, and addressing a large woman, the most important-looking person of the three, as politely as I could, I said I was not, as they perhaps imagined, a long absent friend or relation returned from the wars, but a perfect stranger, a traveller on the great south road; that I was hot and thirsty, and the sight of them refreshing themselves in that pleasant shade had tempted me to intrude myself upon them.

She received me with smiles and a torrent of welcoming words, and the expected invitation to sit down and drink maté with them. She was a very large woman, very fat and very dark, of that reddish or mahogany colour which, taken with the black eyes and coarse black hair, is commonly seen in persons of mixed blood—Iberian with aboriginal. I took her age to be about fifty years. And she was as voluble as she was fat and dark, and poured out such a stream of talk on or rather over me like warm greasy water, and so forcing me to keep my eyes on her, that it was almost impossible to give any attention to the other two. One was her husband, Spanish and dark too, but with a different sort of darkness; a skeleton of a man with a bony ghastly face, in old frayed workman's clothes and dust-covered boots; his hands very grimy. And the third person was their daughter, as they called her, a girl of fifteen with a clear white and pink skin, regular features, beautiful grey eyes and light brown hair. A perfect type of a nice looking English girl such as one finds in any village, in almost any cottage, in the Midlands or anywhere else in this island.

These two were silent, but at length, in one of the fat woman's brief pauses, the girl spoke, in a Spanish in which one could detect no trace of a foreign accent, in a low and pleasing voice, only to say something about the garden. She was strangely earnest and appeared anxious to impress on them that it was necessary to have certain beds of vegetables they cultivated watered that very day lest they should be lost owing to the heat and dryness. The man grunted and the woman said yes, yes, yes, a dozen times. Then the girl left us, going back to her garden, and the fat woman went on talking to me. I tried once or twice to get her to tell me about her daughter, as she called her, but she would not respond—she would at once go off into other subjects. Then I tried something else and told her of my sight of a handsome young lady in mourning I had once seen there feeding the pigeons. And now she responded readily enough and told me the whole story of the lady.

She belonged to a good and very wealthy family of the city and was an only child, and lost both parents when very young. She was a very pretty girl of a joyous nature and a great favourite in society. At the age of sixteen she became engaged to a young man who was also of a good and wealthy family. After becoming engaged to her he went to the war in Paraguay, and after an absence of two years, during which he had distinguished himself in the field and won his captaincy, he returned to marry her. She was at her own house waiting in joyful excitement to receive him when his carriage arrived, and she flew to the door to welcome him. He, seeing her, jumped out and came running to her with his arms out to embrace her, but when still three or four yards distant suddenly stopped short and throwing up his arms fell to the earth a dead man. The shock of his death at this moment of supreme bliss for both of them was more than she could bear; it brought on a fever of the brain and it was feared that if she ever recovered it would be with a shattered mind. But it was not so: she got well and her reason was not lost, but she was changed into a different being from the happy girl of other days—fond of society, of dress, of pleasures; full of life and laughter. "Now she is sadness itself and will continue to wear mourning for the rest of her life, and prefers always to be alone. This old house, built by her grandfather when there were few houses in this suburb, she once liked to visit, but since her loss she has been but once in it. That was when you saw her, when she came to spend a few months in solitude. She would not even allow me to come and sit and talk to her! Think of that! She thinks nothing of her possessions and allows us to live here rent free, to grow vegetables and raise poultry for the market. That is what we do for a living; my husband and our little daughter attend to these things out of doors, and I look after the house."

When she got to the end of this long relation I rose and thanked her for her hospitality and made my escape. But the mystery of the white, gentle-voiced, grey-eyed girl haunted me, and from that time I made it my custom to call at Dovecot House on every journey to town, always to be received with open arms, so to speak, by the great fat woman. But she always baffled me. The girl was usually to be seen, always the same, quiet, unsmiling, silent, or else speaking in Spanish in that gentle un-Spanish voice of some practical matter about the garden, the poultry, and so on. I was not in love with her, but extremely curious to know who she really was and how she came to be a "daughter," or in the hands of these unlikely people. For it was really one of the strangest things I had ever come across up to that early period of my life. Since then I have met with even more curious things; but being then of an age when strange things have a great fascination I was bent on getting to the bottom of the mystery. However, it was in vain; doubtless the fat woman suspected my motives in calling on her and sipping maté and listening to her talk, for whenever I mentioned her daughter in a tentative way, hoping it would lead to talk on that subject, she quickly and skilfully changed it for some other subject. And at last seeing that I was wasting my time, I dropped calling, but to this day I am rather sorry I allowed myself to be defeated.

And now once more I must return for the space of two or three pages to the *brother* white house before saying good-bye to both.

For it had come to pass that while my investigations into the mystery of Dovecot House were in progress I had by chance got my foot in Cannon House. And this is how it happened. When the old Admiral whose ghostly image haunted me had received his message and vanished from this scene, the house was sold and was bought by an Englishman, an old resident in the town, who for thirty years had been toiling and moiling in a business of some kind until he had built a small fortune. It then occurred to him, or more likely his wife and daughters suggested it, that it was time to get a little way out of the hurly-burly, and they accordingly came to live at the house. There were two daughters, tall, slim, graceful girls, one, the elder, dark and pale like her old Cornish father, with black hair; the other a blonde with a rose colour and of a lively merry disposition. These girls happened to be friends of my sisters, and so it fell out that I too became an occasional visitor to Cannon House.

Then a strange thing happened, which made it a sad and anxious home to the inmates for many long months, running to nigh on two years. They were fond of riding, and one afternoon when there was no visitor or any person to accompany them, the youngest girl said she would have her ride and ordered her horse to be brought from the paddock and saddled. Her elder sister, who was of a somewhat timid disposition, tried to dissuade her from riding out alone on the highway. She replied that she would just have one little gallop—a mile or so—and then come back. Her sister, still anxious, followed her out of the gate and said she would wait there for her return. Half a mile or so from the gate the horse, a high-spirited animal, took fright at something and bolted with its rider. The sister waiting and looking out saw them coming, the horse at a furious pace, the rider clinging for dear life to the pummel of the saddle. It flashed on her mind that unless the horse could be stopped before he came crashing through the gate her sister would be killed, and running out to a distance of thirty yards from the gate she jumped at the horse's head as it came rushing by and succeeded in grasping the reins, and holding fast to them she was dragged to within two or three yards of the gate, when the horse was brought to a standstill, whereupon her grasp relaxed and she fell to the ground in a dead faint.

She had done a marvellous thing—almost incredible. I have had horses bolt with me and have seen horses bolt with others many times; and every person who has seen such a thing and who knows a horse—its power and the blind mad terror it is seized with on occasions—will agree with me that it is only at the risk of his life that even a strong and agile man can attempt to stop a bolting horse. We all said that she had saved her sister's life and were lost in admiration of her deed, but presently it seemed that she would pay for it with her own life. She recovered from the faint, but from that day began a decline, until in about three months' time she appeared to me more like a ghost than a being of flesh and blood. She had not strength to cross the rooms—all her strength and life were dying out of her because of that one unnatural, almost supernatural, act. She passed the days lying on a couch, speaking, when obliged to speak, in a whisper, her eyes sunk, her face white even to the lips, seeming the whiter for the mass of loose raven-black hair in which it was set. There were few doctors, English and native, who were not first and last called into consultation over the case, and still no benefit, no return to life, but ever the slow drifting towards the end. And at the last consultation of all this happened. When it was over and the doctors were asked into a room where refreshments were placed for them, the father of the girl spoke aside to a young doctor, a stranger to him, and begged him to tell him truly if there was no hope. The other replied that he should not lose all hope if—then he paused, and when he spoke again it was to say, "I am, you see, a very young man, a beginner in the profession, with little experience, and hardly know why I am called here to consult with these older and wiser men; and naturally my small voice received but little attention."

By-and-by, when they had all gone except the family doctor, he informed the distracted parents that it was impossible to save their daughter's life. The father cried out that he would not lose all hope and would call in another man, whereupon old Dr. Wormwood seized his brass-headed cane and took himself off in a huff. The young stranger was then called in. The patient had been given arsenic with other drugs; he gave her arsenic only, increasing the doses enormously, until she was given as much in a day or two as would have killed a healthy person; with milk for only nourishment. As a result, in a week or so the decline was stayed, and in that condition, very near to dissolution, she continued some weeks, and then slowly, imperceptibly, began to mend. But so slow was the improvement that it went on for months before she was well. It was a complete recovery; she had got back all her old strength and joy in life, and went again for a ride every day with her sister.

Not very long afterwards both sisters were married, and my visits to Cannon House ceased automatically.

Now the two White Houses are but a memory, revived for a brief period to vanish quickly again into oblivion, a something seen long ago and far away in another hemisphere; and they are like two white cliffs seen in passing from the ship at the beginning of its voyage—gazed at with a strange interest as I passed them, and as they receded from me, until they faded from sight in the distance.

IX

DANDY A STORY OF A DOG

He was of mixed breed, and was supposed to have a strain of Dandy Dinmont blood which gave him his name. A big ungainly animal with a rough shaggy coat of blue-grey hair and white on his neck and clumsy paws. He looked like a Sussex sheep-dog with legs reduced to half their proper length. He was, when I first knew him, getting old and increasingly deaf and dim of sight, otherwise in the best of health and spirits, or at all events very good-tempered.

Until I knew Dandy I had always supposed that the story of Ludlam's dog was pure invention, and I daresay that is the general opinion about it; but Dandy made me reconsider the subject, and eventually I came to believe that Ludlam's dog did exist once upon a time, centuries ago perhaps, and that if he had been the laziest dog in the world Dandy was not far behind him in that respect. It is true he did not lean his head against a wall to bark; he exhibited his laziness in other ways. He barked often, though never at strangers; he welcomed every visitor, even the tax-collector, with tail-waggings and a smile. He spent a good deal of his time in the large kitchen, where he had a sofa to sleep on, and when the two cats of the house wanted an hour's rest they would coil themselves up on Dandy's broad shaggy side, preferring that bed to cushion or rug. They were like a warm blanket over him, and it was a sort of mutual benefit society. After an hour's sleep Dandy would go out for a short constitutional as far as the neighbouring thoroughfare, where he would blunder against people, wag his tail to everybody, and then come back. He had six or eight or more outings each day, and, owing to doors and gates being closed and to his lazy disposition, he had much trouble in getting out and in. First he would sit down in the hall and bark, bark, bark, until some one would come to open the door for him, whereupon he would slowly waddle down the garden path, and if he found the gate closed he would again sit down and start barking. And the bark, bark would go on until some one came to let him out. But if after he had barked about twenty or thirty times no one came, he would deliberately open the gate himself, which he could do perfectly well, and let himself out. In twenty minutes or so he would be back at the gate and barking for admission once more, and finally, if no one paid any attention, letting himself in.

Dandy always had something to eat at mealtimes, but he too liked a snack between meals once or twice a day. The dog-biscuits were kept in an open box on the lower dresser shelf, so that he could get one "whenever he felt so disposed," but he didn't like the trouble this arrangement gave him, so he would sit down and start barking, and as he had a bark which was both deep and loud, after it had been repeated a dozen times at intervals of five seconds, any person who happened to be in or near the kitchen was glad to give him his biscuit for the sake of peace and quietness. If no one gave it him, he would then take it out himself and eat it.

Now it came to pass that during the last year of the war dog-biscuits, like many other articles of food for man and beast, grew scarce, and were finally not to be had at all. At all events, that was what happened in Dandy's town of Penzance. He missed his biscuits greatly and often reminded us of it by barking; then, lest we should think he was barking about something else, he would go and sniff and paw at the empty box. He perhaps thought it was pure forgetfulness on the part of those of the house who went every morning to do the marketing and had fallen into the habit of returning without any dog-biscuits in the basket. One day during that last winter of scarcity and anxiety I went to the kitchen and found the floor strewn all over with the fragments of Dandy's biscuit-box. Dandy himself had done it; he had dragged the box from its place out into the middle of the floor, and then deliberately set himself to bite and tear it into small pieces and scatter them about. He was caught at it just as he was finishing the job, and the kindly person who surprised him in the act suggested that the reason of his breaking up the box in that way that he got something of the biscuit flavour by biting the pieces. My own theory was that as the box was there to hold biscuits and now held none, he had come to regard it as useless—as having lost its function, so to speak—also that its presence there was an insult to his intelligence, a constant temptation to make a fool of himself by visiting it half a dozen times a day only to find it empty as usual. Better, then, to get rid of it altogether, and no doubt when he did it he put a little temper into the business!

Dandy, from the time I first knew him, was strictly teetotal, but in former and distant days he had been rather fond of his glass. If a person held up a glass of beer before him, I was told, he wagged his tail in joyful anticipation, and a little beer was always given him at mealtime. Then he had an experience, which, after a little hesitation, I have thought it best to relate, as it is perhaps the most curious incident in Dandy's somewhat uneventful life.

One day Dandy, who after the manner of his kind, had attached himself to the person who was always willing to take him out for a stroll, followed his friend to a neighbouring public-house, where the said friend had to discuss some business matter with the landlord. They went into the taproom, and Dandy, finding that the business was going to be a rather long affair, settled himself down to have a nap. Now it chanced that a barrel of beer which had just been broached had a leaky tap, and the landlord had set a basin on the floor to catch the waste. Dandy, waking from his nap and hearing the trickling sound, got up, and going to the basin quenched his thirst, after which he resumed his nap. By-and-by he woke again and had a second drink, and altogether he woke and had a drink five or six times; then, the business being concluded, they went out together, but no sooner were they in the fresh air than Dandy began to exhibit signs of inebriation. He swerved from side to side, colliding with the passers-by, and finally fell off the pavement into the swift stream of water which at that point runs in the gutter at one side of the street. Getting out of the water, he started again, trying to keep close to the wall to save himself from another ducking. People looked curiously at him, and by-and-by they began to ask what the matter was. "Is your dog going to have a fit—or what is it?" they asked. Dandy's friend said he didn't know; something was the matter no doubt, and he would take him home as quickly as possible and see to it.

When they finally got to the house Dandy staggered to his sofa, and succeeded in climbing on to it and, throwing himself on his cushion, went fast asleep, and slept on without a break until the following morning. Then he rose quite refreshed and appeared to have forgotten all about it; but that day when at dinner-time some one said "Dandy" and held up a glass of beer, instead of wagging his tail as usual he dropped it between his legs and turned away in evident disgust. And from that time onward he would never touch it with his tongue, and it was plain that when they tried to tempt him, setting beer before him and smilingly inviting him to drink, he knew they were mocking him, and before turning away he would emit a low growl and show his teeth. It was the one thing that put him out and would make him angry with his friends and life companions.

I should not have related this incident if Dandy had been alive. But he is no longer with us. He was old—half-way between fifteen and sixteen: it seemed as though he had waited to see the end of the war, since no sooner was the armistice proclaimed than he began to decline rapidly. Gone deaf and blind, he still insisted on taking several constitutionals every day, and would bark as usual at the gate, and if no one came to let him out or admit him, he would open it for himself as before. This went on till January, 1919, when some of the boys he knew were coming back to Penzance and to the house. Then he established himself on his sofa, and we knew that his end was near, for there he would sleep all day and all night, declining food. It is customary in this country to chloroform a dog and give him a dose of strychnine to "put him out of his misery." But it was not necessary in this case, as he was not in misery; not a groan did he ever emit, waking or sleeping; and if you put a hand on him he would look up and wag his tail just to let you know that it was well with him. And in his sleep he passed away—a perfect case of euthanasia—and was buried in the large garden near the second apple-tree.

X

THE SAMPHIRE GATHERER

At sunset, when the strong wind from the sea was beginning to feel cold, I stood on the top of the sandhill looking down at an old woman hurrying about over the low damp ground beneath—a bit of sea-flat divided from the sea by the ridge of sand; and I wondered at her, because her figure was that of a feeble old woman, yet she moved—I had almost said flitted—over that damp level ground in a surprisingly swift light manner, pausing at intervals to stoop and gather something from the surface. But I couldn't see her distinctly enough to satisfy myself: the sun was sinking below the horizon, and that dimness in the air and coldness in the wind at day's decline, when the year too was declining, made all objects look dim. Going down to her I found that she was old, with thin grey hair on an uncovered head, a lean dark face with regular features and grey eyes that were not old and looked steadily at mine, affecting me with a sudden mysterious sadness. For they were unsmiling eyes and themselves expressed an unutterable sadness, as it appeared to me at the first swift glance; or perhaps not that, as it presently seemed, but a shadowy something which sadness had left in them, when all pleasure and all interest in life forsook her, with all affections, and she no longer cherished either memories or hopes. This may be nothing but conjecture or fancy, but if she had been a visitor from another world she could not have seemed more strange to me.

I asked her what she was doing there so late in the day, and she answered in a quiet even voice which had a shadow in it too, that she was gathering samphire of that kind which grows on the flat saltings and has a dull green leek-like fleshy leaf. At this season, she informed me, it was fit for gathering to pickle and put by for use during the year. She carried a pail to put it in, and a table-knife in her hand to dig the plants up by the roots, and she also had an old sack in which she put every dry stick and chip of wood she came across. She added that she had gathered samphire at this same spot every August end for very many years.

I prolonged the conversation, questioning her and listening with affected interest to her mechanical answers, while trying to fathom those unsmiling, unearthly eyes that looked so steadily at mine.

And presently, as we talked, a babble of human voices reached our ears, and half turning we saw the crowd, or rather procession, of golfers coming from the golf-house by the links where they had been drinking tea. Ladies and gentlemen players, forty or more of them, following in a loose line, in couples and small groups, on their way to the Golfers' Hotel, a little further up the coast; a remarkably good-looking lot with well-fed happy faces, well-dressed and in a merry mood, all freely talking and laughing. Some were staying at the hotel, and for the others a score or so of motor-cars were standing before its gates to take them inland to their homes, or to houses where they were staying.

We suspended the conversation while they were passing us, within three yards of where we stood, and as they passed the story of the links where they had been amusing themselves since luncheon-time came into my mind. The land there was owned by an old, an ancient, family; they had occupied it, so it is said, since the Conquest; but the head of the house was now poor, having no house property in London, no coal mines in Wales, no income from any other source than the land, the twenty or thirty thousand acres let for farming. Even so he would not have been poor, strictly speaking, but for the sons, who preferred a life of pleasure in town, where they probably had private establishments of their own. At all events they kept race-horses, and had their cars, and lived in the best clubs, and year by year the patient old father was called upon to discharge their debts of honour. It was a painful position for so estimable a man to be placed in, and he was much pitied by his friends and neighbours, who regarded him as a worthy representative of the best and oldest family in the county. But he was compelled to do what he could to make both ends meet, and one of the little things he did was to establish golf-links over a mile or so of sand-hills, lying between the ancient coast village and the sea, and to build and run a Golfers' Hotel in order to attract visitors from all parts. In this way, incidentally, the villagers were cut off from their old direct way to the sea and deprived of those barren dunes, which were their open space and recreation ground and had stood them in the place of a common for long centuries. They were warned off and told that they must use a path to the beach which took them over half a mile from the village. And they had been very humble and obedient and had made no complaint. Indeed, the agent had assured them that they had every reason to be grateful to the overlord, since in return for that trivial inconvenience they had been put to they would have the golfers there, and there would be employment for some of the village boys as caddies. Nevertheless, I had discovered that they were not grateful but considered that an injustice had been done to them, and it rankled in their hearts.

I remembered all this while the golfers were streaming by, and wondered if this poor woman did not, like her fellow-villagers, cherish a secret bitterness against those who had deprived them of the use of the dunes where for generations they had been accustomed to walk or sit or lie on the loose yellow sands among the barren grasses, and had also cut off their direct way to the sea where they went daily in search of bits of firewood and whatever else the waves threw up which would be a help to them in their poor lives.

If it be so, I thought, some change will surely come into those unchanging eyes at the sight of all these merry, happy golfers on their way to their hotel and their cars and luxurious homes. But though I watched her face closely there was no change, no faintest trace of ill-feeling or feeling of any kind; only that same shadow which had been there was there still, and her fixed eyes were like those of a captive bird or animal, that gaze at us, yet seem not to see us but to look through and beyond us. And it was the same when they had all gone by and we finished our talk and I put money in her hand; she thanked me without a smile, in the same quiet even tone of voice in which she had replied to my question about the samphire.

I went up once more to the top of the ridge, and looking down saw her again as I had seen her at first, only dimmer, swiftly, lightly moving or flitting moth-like or ghost-like over the low flat salting, still gathering samphire in the cold wind, and the thought that came to me was that I was looking at and had been interviewing a being that was very like a ghost, or in any case a soul, a something which could not be described, like certain atmospheric effects in earth and water and sky which are ignored by the landscape painter. To protect himself he cultivates what is called the "sloth of the eye": he thrusts his fingers into his ears so to speak, not to hear that mocking voice that follows and mocks him with his miserable limitations. He who seeks to convey his impressions with a pen is almost as badly off: the most he can do in such instances as the one related, is to endeavour to convey the emotion evoked by what he has witnessed.

Let me then take the case of the man who has trained his eyes, or rather whose vision has unconsciously trained itself, to look at every face he meets, to find in most cases something, however little, of the person's inner life. Such a man could hardly walk the length of the Strand and Fleet-street or of Oxford-street without being startled at the sight of a face which haunts him with its tragedy, its mystery, the strange things it has half revealed. But it does not haunt him long; another arresting face follows, and then another, and the impressions all fade and vanish from the memory in a little while. But from time to time, at long intervals, once perhaps in a lustrum, he will encounter a face that will not cease to haunt him, whose vivid impression will not fade for years. It was a face and eyes of that kind which I met in the samphire gatherer on that cold evening; but the mystery of it is a mystery still.

XI

A SURREY VILLAGE

Through the scattered village of Churt, in its deepest part, runs a clear stream, broad in places, where it spreads over the road-way and is so shallow that the big carthorses are scarce wetted above their fetlocks in crossing; in other parts narrow enough for a man to jump over, yet deep enough for the trout to hide in. And which is the prettiest one finds it hard to say—the wide splashy places where the cattle come to drink, and the real cow and the illusory inverted cow beneath it are to be seen touching their lips; or where the oaks and ashes and elms stretch and mingle their horizontal branches;—where there is a green leafy canopy above and its green reflection below with the glassy current midway between. On one side the stream is Surrey, on the other Hampshire. Where the two counties meet there is a vast extent of heath-land—brown desolate moors and hills so dark as to look almost black.

It is wild, and its wildness is of that kind which comes of a barren soil. It is a country best appreciated by those who, rich or poor, take life easily, who love all aspects of nature, all weathers, and above everything the liberty of wide horizons. To others the cry of "Back to the land" would have a somewhat dreary and mocking sound in such a place, like that curious cry, half laughter and half wail, which the peewit utters as he anxiously winnows the air with creaking wings above the pedestrian's head. But it is not all of this character. From some black hill-top one looks upon a green expanse, fresh and lively by contrast as the young leaves of deciduous trees in spring, with black again or dark brown of pine and heath beyond. It is the oasis where Churt is. The vivifying spirit of the wind at that height, and that vision of verdure beneath, produce an exhilarating effect on the mind. It is common knowledge that the devil once lived in or haunted these parts: now my hill-top fancy tells me that once upon a time a better being, a wandering angel, flew over the country, and looking down and seeing it so dark-hued and desolate, a compassionate impulse took him, and unclasping his light mantle he threw it down, so that the human inhabitants should not be without that sacred green colour that elsewhere beautifies the earth. There to this day it lies where it fell—a mantle of moist vivid green, powdered with silver and gold, embroidered with all floral hues; all reds from the faint blush on the petals of the briar-rose to the deep crimson of the red trifolium; and all yellows, and blues, and purples.

It was pleasant to return from a ramble over the rough heather to the shade of the green village lanes, to stand aside in some deep narrow road to make room for a farmer's waggon to pass, drawn by five or six ponderous horses; to meet the cows too, smelling of milk and new-mown hay, attended by the small cow-boy. One notices in most rural districts how stunted in growth many of the boys of the labourers are; here I was particularly struck by it on account of the fine physique of many of the young men. It is possible that the growing time may be later and more rapid here than in most places. Some of the young men are exceptionally tall, and there was a larger percentage of tall handsome women than I have seen in any village in Surrey and Hampshire. But the children were almost invariably too small for their years. The most stunted specimen was a little boy I met near Hindhead. He was thin, with a dry wizened face, and looked at the most about eight years old; he assured me that he was twelve. I engaged this gnome-like creature to carry something for me, and we had three or four miles ramble together. A curious couple we must have seemed—a giant and a pigmy, the pigmy looking considerably older than the giant. He was a heath-cutter's child, the eldest of seven children! They were very poor, but he could earn nothing himself, except by gathering whortleberries in their season; then he said, all seven of them turned out with their parents, the youngest in its mother's arms. I questioned him about the birds of the district; he stoutly maintained that he recognised only four, and proceeded to name them.

"Here is another," said I, "a fifth you didn't name, singing in the bushes half a dozen yards from where we stand—the best singer of all."

"I did name it," he returned, "that's a thrush."

It was a nightingale, a bird he did not know. But he knew a thrush—it was one of the four birds he knew, and he stuck to it that it was a thrush singing. Afterwards he pointed out the squalid-looking cottage he lived in. It was on the estate of a great lady.

"Tell me," I said, "is she much liked on the estate?"

He pondered the question for a few moments, then replied, "Some likes her and some don't," and not a word more would he say on that subject. A curious amalgam of stupidity and shrewdness; a bad observer of bird-life, but a cautious little person in answering leading questions; he was evidently growing up (or not doing so) in the wrong place.

Going out for a stroll in the evening, I came to a spot where two small cottages stood on one side of the road, and a large pond fringed with rushes and a coppice on the other. Just by the cottage five boys were amusing themselves by throwing stones at a mark, talking, laughing and shouting at their play. Not many yards from the noisy boys some fowls were picking about on the turf close to the pond; presently out of the rushes came a moorhen and joined them. It was in fine feather, very glossy, the brightest nuptial yellow and scarlet on beak and shield. It moved about, heedless of my presence and of the noisy stone-throwing boys, with that pretty dignity and unconcern which make it one of the most attractive birds. What a contrast its appearance and motions presented to those of the rough-hewn, ponderous fowls, among which it moved so daintily! I was about to say that he was "just like a modern gentleman" in the midst of a group of clodhoppers in rough old coats, hob-nailed boots, and wisps of straw round their corduroys, standing with clay pipes in their mouths, each with a pot of beer in his hand. Such a comparison would have been an insult to the moorhen. Nevertheless some ambitious young gentleman of aesthetic tastes might do worse than get himself up in this bird's livery. An open coat of olive-brown silk, with an oblique white band at the side; waistcoat or cummerbund, and knickerbockers, slaty grey; stockings and shoes of olive green; and, for a touch of bright colour, an orange and scarlet tie. It would be pleasant to meet him in Piccadilly. But he would never, never be able to get that quaint pretty carriage. The "Buzzard lope" and the crane's stately stride are imitable by man, but not the moorhen's gait. And what a mess of it our young gentleman would make in attempting at each step to throw up his coat tails in order to display conspicuously the white silk underlining!

While I watched the pretty creature, musing sadly the while on the ugliness of men's garments, a sudden storm of violent rasping screams burst from some holly bushes a few yards away. It proceeded from three excited jays, but whether they were girding at me, the shouting boys, or a skulking cat among the bushes, I could not make out.

When I finally left this curious company—noisy boys, great yellow feather-footed fowls, dainty moorhen and vociferous jays—it was late, but another amusing experience was in store for me. Leaving the village I went up the hill to the Devil's Jumps to see the sun set. The Devil, as I have said, was much about these parts in former times; his habits were quite familiar to the people, and his name became associated with some of the principal landmarks and features of the landscape. It was his custom to go up into these rocks, where, after drawing his long tail over his shoulder to have it out of his way, he would take one of his great flying leaps or jumps. On the opposite side of the village we have the Poor Devil's Bottom—a deep treacherous hole that cuts like a ravine through the moor, into which the unfortunate fellow once fell and broke several of his bones. A little further away, on Hindhead, we have the Devil's Punch Bowl, that huge basin-shaped hollow on the hill which has now become almost as famous as Flamborough Head or the Valley of Rocks.

At the Jumps a shower came on, and to escape a wetting I crept into a hole or hollow in the rude mass of black basaltic rock which stands like a fortress or ruined castle on the summit of the hill. When the shower was nearly over I heard the wing-beats and low guttural voice of a cuckoo; he did not see my crouching form in the hollow and settled on a projecting block of stone close to me—not three yards from my head. Presently he began to call, and it struck me as very curious that his voice did not sound louder or different in quality than when heard at a distance of forty or fifty yards. When he had finished calling and flown away I crept out of my hole and walked back over the wet heath, thinking now of the cuckoo and now of that half natural, half supernatural but not very sublime being who, as I have said, was formerly a haunter of these parts. This was a question that puzzled my mind. It is easy to say that legends of the Devil are common enough all over the land, and date back to old monkish times or to the beginning of Christianity, when the spiritual enemy was very much in man's thoughts; the curious thing is, that the devil associated in tradition with certain singular features in the landscape, as it is here in this Surrey village, and in a thousand other places, has little or no resemblance to the true and only Satan. He is at his greatest a sort of demi-god, or a semi-human being or monster of abnormal power and wildly eccentric habits, but not really bad. Thus, I was told by a native of Churt that when the Devil met with that serious accident which gave its name to the Poor Devil's Bottom, his painful cries and groans attracted the villagers, and they ministered to him, giving him food and drink and applying such remedies as they knew of to his hurts until he recovered and got out of the hole. Whether or not this legend has ever been recorded I cannot say; one is struck with its curious resemblance to some of the giant legends of the west of England. Near Devizes there is a deep impression in the earth about which a very different story is told: it is called the Devil's Jumps and is, I believe, supposed to be an entrance to his subterranean dwelling-place. He jumps down through that hole, the earth opens to receive him, and closes behind him. And it is (or was) believed that if any person will run three times round the hole the Devil will issue from it and start off in chase of a hare! Why he comes forth and chases a hare nobody knows.

It was only recently, when in Cornwall, the most legendary of the counties, that I found out who and what this rural village devil I had been thinking of really was. In Cornwall one finds many legends of the Devil, as many in fact as in Flintshire, where the Devil has left so many memorials on the downs, but they are few to those relating to the giants. These legends were collected by Robert Hunt, and first published over half a century ago in his *Popular Romances of the West of England*, and he points out in this work that "devil" in most of the legends appears to be but another name for "giant," that in many cases the character of the being is practically the same. He believes that traditions of giants, which probably date back to prehistoric times, were once common all over the country, that they were always associated with certain impressive features in the landscape—grotesque hills, chasms and hollows in the downs and huge masses of rock; that the early teachers of Christianity, anxious to kill these traditions, or to blot out a false belief or superstition with the darker and more terrible image of a powerful being at war with man, taught that "giant" was but another name for Devil. If this is so, the teaching was not altogether good policy. The giants, it is true, were an awesome folk and flung immense rocks about in a reckless manner and did many other mad things; and there were some that were wholly bad, just as there are rogue elephants and as there are black sheep in the human flock, but they were not really bad as a rule, and certainly not too intelligent. Even little men with their cunning little brains could get the better of them. The result of such teaching could only be that the Devil would be regarded as not the unmitigated monster they had been told that he was, nor without human weaknesses and virtues. When we say now that he is not "as black as he is painted" we may be merely repeating what was being said by the common people of England in the days of St. Augustine and St. Colomb, and of the Irish missionaries in Cornwall.

XII

A WILTSHIRE VILLAGE

"What is your nearest village?" I asked of a labourer I met on the road one bleak day in early spring, after a great frost: for I had walked far enough and was cold and tired, and it seemed to me that it would be well to find shelter for the night and a place to settle down in for a season.

"Burbage," he answered, pointing the way to it.

And when I came to it, and walked slowly and thoughtfully the entire length of its one long street or road, my sister said to me:

"Yet another old ancient village!" and then, with a slight tremor in her voice, "And you are going to stay in it!"

"Yes," I replied, in a tone of studied indifference: but as to whether it was ancient or not I could not say;—I had never heard its name before, and knew nothing about it: doubtless it was characteristic—"That weary word," she murmured.

—But it was neither strikingly picturesque, nor quaint, nor did I wish it were either one or the other, nor anything else attractive or remarkable, since I sought only for a quiet spot where my brain might think the thoughts and my hand do the work that occupied me. A village remote, rustic, commonplace, that would make no impression on my preoccupied mind and leave no lasting image, nor anything but a faint and fading memory.

> Thus I pacified Psyche and kissed her,
> And tempted her out of her gloom—
> And conquered her scruples and gloom.

And fortune favoured her, all things conspiring to keep me content to walk in that path which I had so readily, so lightly, promised to keep: for the work to be done was bread and cheese to me, and in a sense to her, and had to be done, and there was nothing to distract attention.

It was quiet in my chosen cottage, in the low-ceilinged room where I usually sat: outside, the walls were covered with ivy which made it like a lonely lodge in a wood; and when I opened my small outward-opening latticed window there was no sound except the sighing of the wind in the old yew tree growing beside and against the wall, and at intervals the chirruping of a pair of sparrows that flew up from time to time from the road with long straws in their bills. They were building a nest beneath my window—possibly it was the first nest made that year in all this country.

All the day long it was quiet; and when, tired of work, I went out and away from the village across the wide vacant fields, there was nothing to attract the eye. The deadly frost which had held us for long weeks in its grip had gone, for it was now drawing to the end of March, but winter was still in the air and in the earth. Day after day a dull cloud was over all the sky and the wind blew cold from the north-east. The aspect of the country, as far as one could see in that level plain, was wintry and colourless. The hedges in that part are kept cut and trimmed so closely that they seemed less like hedges than mere faint greyish fences of brushwood, dividing field from field: they would not have afforded shelter to a hedge-sparrow. The trees were few and far apart—grey naked oaks, un-visited even by the tits that find their food in bark and twig; the wide fields between were bare and devoid of life of man or beast or bird. Ploughed and grass lands were equally desolate; for the grass was last year's, long dead and now of that neutral, faded, and palest of all pale dead colours in nature. It is not white nor yellow, and there is no name for it. Looking down when I walked in the fields the young spring grass could be seen thrusting up its blades among the old and dead, but at a distance of a few yards these delicate living green threads were invisible.

Coming back out of the bleak wind it always seemed strangely warm in the village street—it was like coming into a room in which a fire has been burning all day. So grateful did I find this warmth of the deep old sheltered road, so vocal too and full of life did it seem after the pallor and silence of the desolate world without, that I made it my favourite walk, measuring its length from end to end. Nor was it strange that at last, unconsciously, in spite of a preoccupied brain and of the assurance given that I would reside in the village, like a snail in its shell, without seeing it, an impression began to form and an influence to be felt.

Some vague speculations passed through my mind as to how old the village might be. I had heard some person remark that it had formerly been much more populous, that many of its people had from time to time drifted away to the towns; their old empty cottages pulled down and no new ones built. The road was deep and the cottages on either side stood six to eight or nine feet above it. Where a cottage stood close to the edge of the road and faced it, the door was reached by a flight of stone or brick steps; at such cottages the landing above the steps was like a balcony, where one could stand and look down upon a passing cart, or the daily long straggling procession of children going to or returning from the village school. I counted the steps that led up to my own front door and landing place and found there were ten: I took it that each step represented a century's wear of the road by hoof and wheel and human feet, and the conclusion was thus that the village was a thousand years old—probably it was over two thousand. A few centuries more or less did not seem to matter much; the subject did not interest me in the least, my passing thought about it was an idle straw showing which way the mental wind was blowing.

Albeit half-conscious of what that way was, I continued to assure Psyche—my sister—that all was going well: that if she would only keep quiet there would be no trouble, seeing that I knew my own weakness so well—a habit of dropping the thing I am doing because something more interesting always crops up. Here fortunately for us (and our bread and cheese) there was nothing interesting—ab-so-lute-ly.

But in the end, when the work was finished, the image that had been formed could no longer be thrust away and forgotten. It was there, an entity as well as an image—an intelligent masterful being who said to me not in words but very plainly: *Try to ignore me and it will be worse for you: a secret want will continually disquiet you: recognize my existence and right to dwell in and possess your soul, as you dwell in mine, and there will be a pleasant union and peace between us.*

To resist, to argue the matter like some miserable metaphysician would have been useless.

The persistent image was of the old deep road, the green bank on each side, on which stood thatched cottages, whitewashed or of the pale red of old weathered bricks; each with its plot of ground or garden with, in some cases, a few fruit trees. Here and there stood a large shade tree—oak or pine or yew; then a vacant space, succeeded by a hedge, gapped and ragged and bare, or of evergreen holly or yew, smoothly trimmed; then a ploughed field, and again cottages, looking up or down the road, or placed obliquely, or facing it: and looking at one cottage and its surrounding, there would perhaps be a water-butt standing beside it; a spade and fork leaning against the wall; a white cat sitting in the shelter idly regarding three or four fowls moving about at a distance of a few yards, their red feathers ruffled by the wind; further away a wood-pile; behind it a pigsty sheltered by bushes, and on the ground, among the dead weeds, a chopping-block, some broken bricks, little heaps of rusty iron, and other litter. Each plot had its own litter and objects and animals.

On the steeply sloping sides of the road the young grass was springing up everywhere among the old rubbish of dead grass and leaves and sticks and stems. More conspicuous than the grass blades, green as verdigris, were the arrow-shaped leaves of the arum or cuckoo-pint. But there were no flowers yet except the wild strawberry, and these so few and small that only the eager eyes of the little children, seeking for spring, might find them.

Nor was the village less attractive in its sounds than in the natural pleasing disorder of its aspect and the sheltering warmth of its street. In the fields and by the skimpy hedges perfect silence reigned; only the wind blowing in your face filled your ears with a rushing aerial sound like that which lives in a seashell. Coming back from this open bleak silent world, the village street seemed vocal with bird voices. For the birds, too, loved the shelter which had enabled them to live through that great frost; and they were now recovering their voices; and whenever the wind lulled and a gleam of sunshine fell from the grey sky, they were singing from end to end of the long street.

Listening to, and in some instances seeing the singers and counting them, I found that there were two thrushes, four blackbirds, several chaffinches and green finches, one pair of goldfinches, half-a-dozen linnets and three or four yellow-hammers; a sprinkling of hedge-sparrows, robins and wrens all along the street; and finally, one skylark from a field close by would rise and sing at a considerable height directly above the road. Gazing up at the lark and putting myself in his place, the village beneath with its one long street appeared as a vari-coloured band lying across the pale earth. There were dark and bright spots, lines and streaks, of yew and holly, red or white cottage walls and pale yellow thatch; and the plots and gardens were like large reticulated mottlings. Each had its centre of human life with life of bird and beast, and the centres were in touch with one another, connected like a row of children linked together by their hands; all together forming one organism, instinct with one life, moved by one mind, like a many-coloured serpent lying at rest, extended at full length upon the ground.

I imagined the case of a cottager at one end of the village occupied in chopping up a tough piece of wood or stump and accidentally letting fall his heavy sharp axe on to his foot, inflicting a grievous wound. The tidings of the accident would fly from mouth to mouth to the other extremity of the village, a mile distant; not only would every individual quickly know of it, but have at the same time a vivid mental image of his fellow villager at the moment of his misadventure, the sharp glittering axe falling on to his foot, the red blood flowing from the wound; and he would at the same time feel the wound in his own foot, and the shock to his system.

In like manner all thoughts and feelings would pass freely from one to another, although not necessarily communicated by speech; and all would be participants in virtue of that sympathy and solidarity uniting the members of a small isolated community. No one would be capable of a thought or emotion which would seem strange to the others. The temper, the mood, the outlook, of the individual and the village would be the same.

I remember that something once occurred in a village where I was staying, which was in a way important to the villagers, although it gave them nothing and took nothing from them: it excited them without being a question of politics, or of "morality," to use the word in its narrow popular sense. I spoke first to a woman of the village about it, and was not a little surprised at the view she took of the matter, for to me this seemed unreasonable; but I soon found that all the villagers took this same unreasonable view, their indignation, pity and other emotions excited being all expended as it seemed to me in the wrong direction. The woman had, in fact, merely spoken the mind of the village.

Owing to this close intimacy and family character of the village which continues from generation to generation, there must be under all differences on the surface a close mental likeness hardly to be realised by those who live in populous centres; a union between mind and mind corresponding to that reticulation as it appeared to me, of plot with plot and with all they contained. It is perhaps equally hard to realise that this one mind of a particular village is individual, wholly its own, unlike that of any other village, near or far. For one village differs from another; and the village is in a sense a body, and this body and the mind that inhabits it, act and react on one another, and there is between them a correspondence and harmony, although it may be but a rude harmony.

It is probable that we that are country born and bred are affected in more ways and more profoundly than we know by our surroundings. The nature of the soil we live on, the absence or presence of running water, of hills, rocks, woods, open spaces; every feature in the landscape, the vegetative and animal life—everything in fact that we see, hear, smell and feel, enters not into the body only, but the soul, and helps to shape and colour it. Equally important in its action on us are the conditions created by man himself:—situation, size, form and the arrangements of the houses in the village; its traditions, customs and social life.

On that airy *mirador* which I occupied under (not in) the clouds, after surveying the village beneath me I turned my sight abroad and saw, near and far, many many other villages; and there was no other exactly like Burbage nor any two really alike.

Each had its individual character. To mention only two that were nearest— East Grafton and Easton, or Easton Royal. The first, small ancient rustic-looking place: a large green, park-like shaded by well-grown oak, elm, beech, and ash trees; a small slow stream of water winding through it: round this pleasant shaded and watered space the low-roofed thatched cottages, each cottage in its own garden, its porch and walls overgrown with ivy and creepers. Thus, instead of a straight line like Burbage it formed a circle, and every cottage opened on to the tree-shaded village green; and this green was like a great common room where the villagers meet, where the children play, where lovers whisper their secrets, where the aged and weary take their rest, and all subjects of interest are daily discussed. If a blackcap or chaffinch sung in one of the trees the strain could be heard in every cottage in the circle. All hear and see the same things, and think and feel the same.

The neighbouring village was neither line, nor circle, but a cluster of cottages. Or rather a group of clusters, so placed that a dozen or more housewives could stand at their respective doors, very nearly facing one another, and confabulate without greatly raising their voices. Outside, all round, the wide open country

—grass and tilled land and hedges and hedgerow elms—is spread out before them. And in sight of all the cottages, rising a little above them, stands the hoary ancient church with giant old elm-trees growing near it, their branches laden with rooks' nests, the air full of the continuous noise of the wrangling birds, as they fly round and round, and go and come bringing sticks all day, one to add to the high airy city, the other to drop as an offering to the earth-god beneath, in whose deep-buried breast the old trees have their roots.

But the other villages that cannot be named were in scores and hundreds, scattered all over Wiltshire, for the entire county was visible from that altitude, and not Wiltshire only but Somerset, and Berkshire and Hampshire, and all the adjoining counties, and finally, the prospect still widening, all England from rocky Land's End to the Cheviots and the wide windy moors sprinkled over with grey stone villages. Thousands and thousands of villages; but I could only see a few distinctly—not more than about two hundred, the others from their great distance—not in space but time—appearing but vaguely as spots of colour on the earth. Then, fixing my attention on those that were most clearly seen, I found myself in thought loitering in them, revisiting cottages and conversing with old people and children I knew; and recalling old and remembered scenes and talks, I smiled and by-and-by burst out laughing.

It was then, when I laughed, that visions, dreams, memories, were put to flight, for my wise sister was studying my face, and now, putting her hand on mine, she said, "Listen!" And I listened, sadly, since I could guess what was coming.

"I know," she said, "just what is at the back of your mind, and all these innumerable villages you are amusing yourself by revisiting, is but a beginning, a preliminary canter. For not only is it the idea of the village and the mental colour in which it dyes its children's mind which fades never, however far they may go, though it may be to die at last in remote lands and seas—"

Here I interrupted, "O yes! Do you remember a poet's lines to the little bourne in his childhood's home? A poet in that land where poetry is a rare plant—I mean Scotland. I mean the lines:

> How men that niver have kenned aboot it
> Can lieve their after lives withoot it
> I canna tell, for day and nicht
> It comes unca'd for to my sicht."

"Yes," she replied, smiling sadly, and then, mocking my bad Scotch, "and do ye ken that ither one, a native too of that country where, as you say, poetry is a rare plant; that great wanderer over many lands and seas, seeker after summer everlasting, who died thousands of miles from home in a tropical island, and was borne to his grave on a mountain top by the dark-skinned barbarous islanders, weeping and lamenting their dead Tusitala, and the lines he wrote—do you remember?

> Be it granted to me to behold you again in dying,
> Hills of my home! and to hear again the call—
> Hear about the graves of the martyrs, the pee-wees crying,
> And hear no more at all!"

"Oh, I was foolish to quote those lines on a Scotch burn to you, knowing how you would take such a thing up! For you are the very soul of sadness—a sadness that is like a cruelty—and for all your love, my sister, you would have killed me with your sadness had I not refused to listen so many many times!"

"No! No! No! Listen now to what I had to say without interrupting me again: All this about the villages, viewed from up there where the lark sings, is but a preliminary—a little play to deceive yourself and me. For, all the time you are thinking of other things, serious and some exceedingly sad—of those who live not in villages but in dreadful cities, who are like motherless men who have never known a mother's love and have never had a home on earth. And you are like one who has come upon a cornfield, ripe for the harvest with you alone to reap it. And viewing it you pluck an ear of corn, and rub the grains out in the palm of your hand, and toss them up, laughing and playing with them like a child, pretending you are thinking of nothing, yet all the time thinking—thinking of the task before you. And presently you will take to the reaping and reap until the sun goes down, to begin again at sunrise to toil and sweat again until evening. Then, lifting your bent body with pain and difficulty, you will look to see how little you have done, and that the field has widened and now stretches away before you to the far horizon. And in despair you will cast the sickle away and abandon the task."

"What then, O wise sister, would you have me do?"

"Leave it now, and save yourself this fresh disaster and suffering."

"So be it! I cannot but remember that there have been many disasters—more than can be counted on the fingers of my two hands—which I would have saved myself if I had listened when I turned a deaf ear to you. But tell me, do you mind just a little more innocent play on my part—just a little picture of, say, one of the villages viewed a while ago from under the cloud—or perhaps two?"

And Psyche, my sister, having won *her* point and pacified me, and conquered my scruples and gloom, and seeing me now submissive, smiled a gracious consent.

XIII

HER OWN VILLAGE

One afternoon when cycling among the limestone hills of Derbyshire I came to an unlovely dreary-looking little village named Chilmorton. It was an exceptionally hot June day and I was consumed with thirst: never had I wanted tea so badly. Small gritstone-built houses and cottages of a somewhat sordid aspect stood on either side of the street, but there was no shop of any kind and not a living creature could I see. It was like a village of the dead or sleeping. At the top of the street I came to the church standing in the middle of its church yard with the public-house for nearest neighbour. Here there was life. Going in I found it the most squalid and evil-smelling village pub I had ever entered. Half a dozen grimy-looking labourers were drinking at the bar, and the landlord was like them in appearance, with his dirty shirt-front open to give his patrons a view of his hairy sweating chest. I asked him to get me tea. "Tea!" he shouted, staring at me as if I had insulted him; "There's no tea here!" A little frightened at his aggressive manner I then meekly asked for soda-water, which he gave me, and it was warm and tasted like a decoction of mouldy straw. After taking a sip and paying for it I went to look at the church, which I was astonished to find open.

It was a relief to be in that cool, twilight, not unbeautiful interior after my day in the burning sun.

After resting and taking a look round I became interested in watching and listening to the talk of two other visitors who had come in before me. One was a slim, rather lean brown-skinned woman, still young but with the incipient crow's-feet, the lines on the forehead, the dusty-looking dark hair, and other signs of time and toil which almost invariably appear in the country labourer's wife before she attains to middle age. She was dressed in a black gown, presumably her best although it was getting a little rusty. Her companion was a fat, red-cheeked young girl in a towny costume, a straw hat decorated with bright flowers and ribbons, and a string of big coloured beads about her neck.

In a few minutes they went out, and when going by me I had a good look at the woman's face, for it was turned towards me with an eager questioning look in her dark eyes and a very friendly smile on her lips. What was the attraction I suddenly found in that sunburnt face?—what did it say to me or remind me of?—what did it suggest?

I followed them out to where they were standing talking among the gravestones, and sitting down on a tomb near them spoke to the woman. She responded readily enough, apparently pleased to have some one to talk to, and pretty soon began to tell me the history of their lives. She told me that Chilmorton was her native place, but that she had been absent from it many many years. She knew just how many years because her child was only six months old when she left and was now fourteen though she looked more. She was such a big girl! Then her man took them to his native place in Staffordshire, where they had lived ever since. But their girl didn't live with them now. An aunt, a sister of her husband, had taken her to the town where she lived, and was having her taught at a private school. As soon as she left school her aunt hoped to get her a place in a draper's shop. For a long time past she had wanted to show her daughter her native place, but had never been able to manage it because it was so far to come and they didn't have much money to spend; but now at last she had brought her and was showing her everything.

Glancing at the girl who stood listening but with no sign of interest in her face, I remarked that her daughter would perhaps hardly think the journey had been worth taking.

"Why do you say that?" she quickly demanded.

"Oh well," I replied, "because Chilmorton can't have much to interest a girl living in a town." Then I foolishly went on to say what I thought of Chilmorton. The musty taste of that warm soda-water was still in my mouth and made me use some pretty strong words.

At that she flared up and desired me to know that in spite of what I thought it Chilmorton was the sweetest, dearest village in England; that she was born there and hoped to be buried in its churchyard where her parents were lying, and her grandparents and many others of her family. She was thirty-six years old now, she said, and would perhaps live to be an old woman, but it would make her miserable for all the rest of her life if she thought she would have to lie in the earth at a distance from Chilmorton.

During this speech I began to think of the soft reply it would now be necessary for me to make, when, having finished speaking, she called sharply to her daughter, "Come, we've others to see yet," and, followed by the girl, walked briskly away without so much as a good-bye, or even a glance!

Oh you poor foolish woman, thought I; why take it to heart like that! and I was sorry and laughed a little as I went back down the street. It was beginning to wake up now! A man in his shirt sleeves and without a hat, a big angry man, was furiously hunting a rebellious pig all round a small field adjoining a cottage, trying to corner it; he swore and shouted, and out of the cottage came a frowsy-looking girl in a ragged gown with her hair hanging all over her face, to help him with the pig. A little further on I caught sight of yet another human being, a tall gaunt old woman in cap and shawl, who came out of a cottage and moved feebly towards a pile of faggots a few yards from the door. Just as she got to the pile I passed, and she slowly turned and gazed at me out of her dim old eyes. Her wrinkled face was the colour of ashes and was like the face of a corpse, still bearing on it the marks of suffering endured for many miserable years. And these three were the only inhabitants I saw on my way down the street.

At the end of the village the street broadened to a clean white road with high ancient hedgerow elms on either side, their upper branches meeting and forming a green canopy over it. As soon as I got to the trees I stopped and dismounted to enjoy the delightful sensation the shade produced: there out of its power I could best appreciate the sun shining in splendour on the wide green hilly earth and in the green translucent foliage above my head. In the upper branches a blackbird was trolling out his music in his usual careless leisurely manner; when I stopped under it the singing was suspended for half a minute or so, then resumed, but in a lower key, which made it seem softer, sweeter, inexpressibly beautiful.

There are beautiful moments in our converse with nature when all the avenues by which nature comes to our souls seem one, when hearing and seeing and smelling and feeling are one sense, when the sweet sound that falls from a bird, is but the blue of heaven, the green of earth, and the golden sunshine made audible.

Such a moment was mine, as I stood under the elms listening to the blackbird. And looking back up the village street I thought of the woman in the churchyard, her sun-parched eager face, her questioning eyes and friendly smile: what was the secret of its attraction?—what did that face say to me or remind me of?—what did it suggest?

Now it was plain enough. She was still a child at heart, in spite of those marks of time and toil on her countenance, still full of wonder and delight at this wonderful world of Chilmorton set amidst its limestone hills, under the wide blue sky—this poor squalid little village where I couldn't get a cup of tea!

It was the child surviving in her which had attracted and puzzled me; it does not often shine through the dulling veil of years so brightly. And as she now appeared to me as a child in heart I could picture her as a child in years, in her little cotton frock and thin bare legs, a sunburnt little girl of eight, with the wide-eyed, eager, half-shy, half-trustful look, asking you, as the child ever asks, what you think?—what you feel? It was a wonderful world, and the world was the village, its streets of gritstone houses, the people living in them, the comedies and tragedies of their lives and deaths, and burials in the churchyard with grass and flowers to grow over them by-and-by. And the church;—I think its interior must have seemed vaster, more beautiful and sublime to her wondering little soul than the greatest cathedral can be to us. I think that our admiration for the loveliest blooms—the orchids and roses and chrysanthemums at our great annual shows—is a poor languid feeling compared to what she experienced at the sight of any common flower of the field. Best of all perhaps were the elms at the village end, those mighty rough-barked trees that had their tops "so close against the sky." And I think that when a blackbird chanced to sing in the upper branches it was as if some angelic being had dropped down out of the sky into that green translucent cloud of leaves, and seeing the child's eager face looking up had sung a little song of his own celestial country to please her.

XIV

APPLE BLOSSOMS AND A LOST VILLAGE

The apple has not come to its perfection this season until the middle of May; even here, in this west country, the very home of the spirit of the apple tree! Now it is, or seems, all the more beautiful because of its lateness, and of an April of snow and sleet and east winds, the bitter feeling of which is hardly yet out of our blood. If I could recover the images of all the flowering apple trees I have ever looked delightedly at, adding those pictured by poets and painters, including that one beneath which Fiammetta is standing, forever, with that fresh glad face almost too beautiful for earth, looking out as from pink and white clouds of the multitudinous blossoms—if I could see all that, I could not find a match for one of the trees of to-day. It is like nothing in earth, unless we say that, indescribable in its loveliness, it is like all other sights in nature which wake in us a sense of the supernatural.

Undoubtedly the apple trees seem more beautiful to us than all other blossoming trees, in all lands we have visited, just because it is so common, so universal—I mean in this west country—so familiar a sight to everyone from infancy, on which account it has more associations of a tender and beautiful kind than the others. For however beautiful it may be intrinsically, the greatest share of the charm is due to the memories that have come to be part of and one with it—the forgotten memories they may be called. For they mostly refer to a far period in our lives, to our early years, to days and events that were happy and sad. The events themselves have faded from the mind, but they registered an emotion, cumulative in its effect, which endures and revives from time to time and is that indefinable feeling, that tender melancholy and "divine despair," and those idle tears of which the poet says, "I know not what they mean," which gather to the eyes at the sight of happy autumn fields and of all lovely natural sights familiar from of old.

To-day, however, looking at the apple blooms, I find the most beautifying associations and memories not in a far-off past, but in visionary apple trees seen no longer ago than last autumn!

And this is how it comes about. In this red and green country of Devon I am apt to meet with adventures quite unlike those experienced in other counties, only they are mostly adventures of the spirit.

Lying awake at six o'clock last October, in Exeter, and seeing it was a grey misty morning, my inclination was to sleep again. I only dozed and was in the twilight condition when the mind is occupied with idle images and is now in the waking world, now in dreamland. A thought of the rivers in the red and green country floated through my brain—of the Clyst among others; then of the villages on the Clyst; of Broadclyst, Clyst St. Mary, Clyst St. Lawrence, finally of Clyst Hyden; and although dozing I half laughed to remember how I went searching for that same village last May and how I wouldn't ask my way of anyone, just because it was Clyst Hyden, because the name of that little hidden rustic village had been written in the hearts of some who had passed away long ago, far far from home:—how then could I fail to find it?—it would draw my feet like a magnet!

I remembered how I searched among deep lanes, beyond rows and rows of ancient hedgerow elms, and how I found its little church and thatched cottages at last, covered with ivy and roses and creepers, all in a white and pink cloud of apple blossoms. Searching for it had been great fun and finding it a delightful experience; why not have the pleasure once more now that it was May again and the apple orchards in blossom? No sooner had I asked myself the question than I was on my bicycle among those same deep lanes, with the unkept hedges and the great hedgerow elms shutting out a view of the country, searching once more for the village of Clyst Hyden. And as on the former occasion, years ago it seemed, I would not enquire my way of anyone. I had found it then for myself and was determined to do so again, although I had set out with the vaguest idea as to the right direction.

But hours went by and I could not find it, and now it was growing late. Through a gap in the hedge I saw the great red globe of the sun quite near the horizon, and immediately after seeing it I was in a narrow road with a green border, which stretched away straight before me further than I could see. Then the thatched cottages of a village came into sight; all were on one side of the road, and the setting sun flamed through the trees had kindled road and trees and cottages to a shining golden flame.

"This is it!" I cried. "This is my little lost village found again, and it is well I found it so late in the day, for now it looks less like even the loveliest old village in Devon than one in fairyland, or in Beulah."

When I came near it that sunset splendour did not pass off and it was indeed like no earthly village; then people came out from the houses to gaze at me, and they too were like people glorified with the sunset light and their faces shone as they advanced hurriedly to meet me, pointing with their hands and talking and laughing excitedly as if my arrival among them had been an event of great importance. In a moment they surrounded and crowded round me, and sitting still among them looking from radiant face to face I at length found my speech and exclaimed, "O how beautiful!"

Then a girl pressed forward from among the others, and putting up her hand she placed it on my temple, the fingers resting on my forehead; and gazing with a strange earnestness in my eyes she said: "Beautiful?—only that! Do you see nothing more?"

I answered, looking back into her eyes: "Yes—I think there is something more but I don't know what it is. Does it come from you—your eyes—your voice, all this that is passing in my mind?"

"What is passing in your mind?" she asked.

"I don't know. Thoughts—perhaps memories: hundreds, thousands—they come and go like lightning so that I can't arrest them—not even one!"

She laughed, and the laugh was like her eyes and her voice and the touch of her hand on my temples.

Was it sad or glad? I don't know, but it was the most beautiful sound I had ever heard, yet it seemed familiar and stirred me in the strangest way.

"Let me think," I said.

"Yes, think!" they all together cried laughingly; and then instantly when I cast my eyes down there was a perfect stillness as if they were all holding their breath and watching me.

That sudden strange stillness startled me: I lifted my eyes and they were gone—the radiant beautiful people who had surrounded and interrogated me, and with them their shining golden village, had all vanished. There was no village, no deep green lanes and pink and white clouds of apple blossoms, and it was not May, it was late October and I was lying in bed in Exeter seeing through the window the red and grey roofs and chimneys and pale misty white sky.

XV

THE VANISHING CURTSEY

'Tis impossible not to regret the dying out of the ancient, quaintly-pretty custom of curtseying in rural England; yet we cannot but see the inevitableness of it, when we consider the earthward drop of the body—the bird-like gesture pretty to see in the cottage child, not so spontaneous nor pretty in the grown girl, and not pretty nor quaint, but rather grotesque (as we think now) in the middle-aged or elderly person—and that there is no longer a corresponding self-abasement and worshipping attitude in the village mind. It is a sign or symbol that has lost, or is losing, its significance.

I have been rambling among a group of pretty villages on and near the Somerset Avon, some in that county, others in Wiltshire; and though these small rustic centres, hidden among the wooded hills, had an appearance of antiquity and of having continued unchanged for very many years, the little ones were as modern in their speech and behaviour as town children. Of all those I met and, in many instances, spoke to, in the village street and in the neighbouring woods and lanes, not one little girl curtseyed to me. The only curtsey I had dropped to me in this district was from an old woman in the small hill-hidden village of Englishcombe. It was on a frosty afternoon in February, and she stood near her cottage gate with nothing on her head, looking at the same time very old and very young. Her eyes were as blue and bright as a child's, and her cheeks were rosy-red; but the skin was puckered with innumerable wrinkles as in the very old. Surprised at her curtsey I stopped to speak to her, and finally went into her cottage and had tea and made the acquaintance of her husband, a gaunt old man with a face grey as ashes and dim colourless eyes, whom Time had made almost an imbecile, and who sat all day groaning by the fire. Yet this worn-out old working man was her junior by several years. Her age was eighty-four. She was very good company, certainly the brightest and liveliest of the dozen or twenty octogenarians I am acquainted with. I heard the story of her life,—that long life in the village where she was born and had spent sixty-five years of married life, and where she would lie in the churchyard with her mate. Her Christian name, she mentioned, was Priscilla, and it struck me that she must have been a very pretty and charming Priscilla about the thirties of the last century.

To return to the little ones; it was too near Bath for such a custom to survive among them, and it is the same pretty well everywhere; you must go to a distance of ten or twenty miles from any large town, or a big station, to meet with curtseying children. Even in villages at a distance from towns and railroads, in purely agricultural districts, the custom is dying out, if, for some reason, strangers are often seen in the place. Such a village is Selborne, and an amusing experience I met with there some time ago serves to show that the old rustic simplicity of its inhabitants is now undergoing a change.

I was walking in the village street with a lady friend when we noticed four little girls coming towards us with arms linked. As they came near they suddenly stopped and curtseyed all together in an exaggerated manner, dropping till their knees touched the ground, then springing to their feet they walked rapidly away. From the bold, free, easy way in which the thing was done it was plain to see that they had been practising the art in something of a histrionic spirit for the benefit of the pilgrims and strangers frequently seen in the village, and for their own amusement. As the little Selbornians walked off they glanced back at us over their shoulders, exhibiting four roguish smiles on their four faces. The incident greatly amused us, but I am not sure that the Reverend Gilbert White would have regarded it in the same humorous light.

Occasionally one even finds a village where strangers are not often seen, which has yet outlived the curtsey. Such a place, I take it, is Alvediston, the small downland village on the upper waters of the Ebble, in southern Wiltshire. One day last summer I was loitering near the churchyard, when a little girl, aged about eight, came from an adjoining copse with some wild flowers in her hand. She was singing as she walked and looked admiringly at the flowers she carried; but she could see me watching her out of the corners of her eyes.

"Good morning," said I. "It is nice to be out gathering flowers on such a day, but why are you not in school?"

"Why am I not in school?" in a tone of surprise. "Because the holidays are not over. On Monday we open."

"How delighted you will be."

"Oh no, I don't *think* I shall be delighted," she returned. Then I asked her for a flower, and apparently much amused she presented me with a water forget-me-not, then she sauntered on to a small cottage close by. Arrived there, she turned round and faced me, her hand on the gate, and after gazing steadily for some moments exclaimed, "Delighted at going back to school—who ever heard such a thing?" and, bursting into a peal of musical child-laughter, she went into the cottage.

One would look for curtseys in the Flower Walk in Kensington Gardens as soon as in the hamlet of this remarkably self-possessed little maid. Her manner was exceptional; but, if we must lose the curtsey, and the rural little ones cease to mimic that pretty drooping motion of the nightingale, the kitty wren, and wheatear, cannot our village pastors and masters teach them some less startling and offensive form of salutation than the loud "Hullo!" with which they are accustomed to greet the stranger within their gates?

I shall finish with another story which might be entitled "The Democrat against Curtseying." The scene was a rustic village, a good many miles from any railroad station, in the south of England. Here I made the acquaintance and was much in the society of a man who was not a native of the place, but had lived several years in it. Although only a working man, he had, by sheer force of character, made himself a power in the village. A total abstainer and non-smoker, a Dissenter in religion and lay-preacher where Dissent had never found a foothold until his coming, and an extreme Radical in politics, he was naturally something of a thorn in the side of the vicar and of the neighbouring gentry.

But in spite of his extreme views and opposition to old cherished ideas and conventions, he was so liberal-minded, so genial in temper, so human, that he was very much liked even by those who were his enemies on principle; and they were occasionally glad to have his help and to work with him in any matter that concerned the welfare of the very poor in the village.

After the first bitterness between him and the important inhabitants had been outlived and a *modus vivendi* established, the vicar ventured one day to remonstrate with the good but mistaken man on the subject of curtseying, which had always been strictly observed in the village. The complaint was that the parishioner's wife did not curtsey to the vicaress, but on the contrary, when she met or passed her on the road she maintained an exceedingly stiff, erect attitude, which was not right, and far from pleasant to the other.

"Is it then your desire," said my democratic friend, "that my wife shall curtsey to your wife when they meet or pass each other in the village?"

"Certainly, that is my wish," said the vicar.

"Very well," said the other; "my wife is guided by me in such matters, and I am very happy to say that she is an obedient wife, and I shall tell her that she is to curtsey to your wife in future."

"Thank you," said the vicar, "I am glad that you have taken it in a proper spirit."

"But I have not yet finished," said the other. "I was going to add that this command to my wife to curtsey to your wife will be made by me on the understanding that you will give a similar command to your wife, and that when they meet and my wife curtseys to your wife, your wife shall at the same time curtsey to my wife."

The vicar was naturally put out and sharply told his rebellious parishioner that he was setting himself against the spirit of the teaching of the Master whom they both acknowledged, and who commanded us to give to everyone his due, with more to the same effect. But he failed to convince, and there was no curtseying.

It was sometimes pleasant and amusing to see these two—the good old clergyman, weak and simple-minded, and his strong antagonist, the aggressive working man with his large frame and genial countenance and great white flowing beard—a Walt Whitman in appearance—working together for some good object in the village. It was even more amusing, but touching as well, to witness an unexpected meeting between the two wives, perhaps at the door of some poor cottage, to which both had gone on the same beautiful errand of love and compassion to some stricken soul, and exchanging only a short "Good-day," the democrat's wife stiffening her knee-joints so as to look straighter and taller than usual.

XVI

LITTLE GIRLS I HAVE MET

Perhaps some reader who does not know a little girl her psychology, after that account of the Alvediston maidie who presented me with a flower with an arch expression on her face just bordering on a mocking smile, will say, "What a sophisticated child to be sure!" He would be quite wrong unless we can say that the female child is born sophisticated, which sounds rather like a contradiction in terms. That appearance of sophistication, common in little girls even in a remote rustic village hidden away among the Wiltshire downs, is implicit in, and a quality of the child's mind—the *female* child, it will be understood—and is the first sign of the flirting instinct which shows itself as early as the maternal one. This, we know, appears as soon as a child is able to stand on its feet, perhaps even before it quits the cradle. It seeks to gratify itself by mothering something, even an inanimate something, so that it is as common to put a doll in a baby-child's hands as it is to put a polished cylindrical bit of ivory—I forget the name of it—in its mouth. The child grows up nursing this image of itself, whether with or without a wax face, blue eyes and tow-coloured hair, and if or when the unreality of the doll begins to spoil its pleasure, it will start mothering something with life in it—a kitten for preference, and if no kitten, or puppy or other such creature easy to be handled or cuddled, is at hand, it will take kindly to any mild-mannered old gentleman of its circle.

It is just these first instinctive impulses of the girl-child, combined with her imitativeness and wonderful precocity, which make her so fascinating. But do they think? They do, but this first early thinking does not make them self-conscious as does their later thinking, to the spoiling of their charm. The thinking indeed begins remarkably early. I remember one child, a little five-year-old and one of my favourites, climbing to my knee one day and exhibiting a strangely grave face. "Doris, what makes you look so serious?" I asked. And after a few moments of silence, during which she appeared to be thinking hard, she startled me by asking me what was the use of living, and other questions which it almost frightened me to hear from those childish innocent lips. Yet I have seen this child grow up to womanhood—a quite commonplace conventional woman, who when she has a child of her own of five would be unspeakably shocked to hear from it the very things she herself spoke at that tender age. And if I were to repeat to her now the words she spoke (the very thought of Byron in his know-that-whatever-thou-hast-been-'Twere-something-better-not-to-be poem) she would not believe it.

It is, however, rare for the child mind in its first essays at reflection to take so far a flight. It begins as a rule like the fledgling by climbing with difficulty out of the nest and on to the nearest branches.

It is interesting to observe these first movements. Quite recently I met with a child of about the same age as the one just described, who exhibited herself to me in the very act of trying to climb out of the nest—trying to grasp something with her claws, so to speak, and pull herself up. She was and is a very beautiful child, full of life and fun and laughter, and came out to me when I was sitting on the lawn to ask me for a story.

"Very well," I said. "But you must wait for half an hour until I remember all about it before I begin. It is a long story about things that happened a long time ago."

She waited as patiently as she could for about three minutes, and then said: "What do you mean by a long time ago?"

I explained, but could see that I had not made her understand, and at last put it in days, then weeks, then seasons, then years, until she appeared to grasp the meaning of a year, and then finished by saying a long time ago in this case meant a hundred years.

Again she was at a loss, but still trying to understand she asked me:
"What is a hundred years?"

"Why, it's a hundred years," I replied. "Can you count to a hundred?"

"I'll try," she said, and began to count and got to nineteen, then stopped. I prompted her, and she went on to twenty-nine, and so on, hesitating after each nine, until she reached fifty. "That's enough," I said, "it's too hard to go the whole way; but now don't you begin to understand what a hundred years means?"

She looked at me and then away, and her beautiful blue intelligent eyes told me plainly that she did not, and that she felt baffled and worried.

After an interval she pointed to the hedge. "Look at the leaves," she said. "I could go and count a hundred leaves, couldn't I? Well, would that be a hundred years?"

And no further could we get, since I could not make out just what the question meant. At first it looked as if she thought of the leaves as an illustration—or a symbol; and then that she had failed to grasp the idea of time, or that it had slipped from her, and she had fallen back, as it were, to the notion that a hundred meant a hundred objects, which you could see and feel. There appeared to be no way out of the puzzle-dom into which we had both got, so that it came as a relief to both of us when she heard her mother calling—calling her back into a world she could understand.

I believe that when we penetrate to the real mind of girl children we find a strong likeness in them even when they appear to differ as widely from one another as adults do. The difference in the little ones is less in disposition and character than in unlikeness due to unconscious imitation. They take their mental colour from their surroundings. The red men of America are the gravest people on the globe, and their children are like them when with them; but this unnatural gravity is on the surface and is a mask which drops or fades off when they assemble together out of sight and hearing of their elders. In like manner our little ones have masks to fit the character of the homes they are bred in.

Here I recall a little girl I once met when I was walking somewhere on the borders of Dorset and Hampshire. It was at the close of an autumn day, and I was on a broad road in a level stretch of country with the low buildings of a farmhouse a quarter of a mile ahead of me, and no other building in sight. A lonely land with but one living creature in sight—a very small girl, slowly coming towards me, walking in the middle of the wet road; for it had been raining a greater part of the day. It was amazing to see that wee solitary being on the lonely road, with the wide green and brown earth spreading away to the horizon on either side under the wide pale sky. She was a sturdy little thing of about five years old, in heavy clothes and cloth cap, and long knitted muffler wrapped round her neck and crossed on her chest, then tied or bound round her waist, thick boots and thick leggings! And she had a round serious face, and big blue eyes with as much wonder in them at seeing me as I suppose mine expressed at seeing her. When we were still a little distance apart she drew away to the opposite side of the road, thinking perhaps that so big a man would require the whole of its twenty-five yards width for himself. But no, that was not the reason of her action, for on gaining the other side she stopped and turned so as to face me when I should be abreast of her, and then at the proper moment she bent her little knees and dropped me an elaborate curtsey; then, rising again to her natural height, she continued regarding me with those wide-open astonished eyes! Nothing in little girls so deliciously quaint and old-worldish had ever come in my way before; and though it was late in the day and the road long, I could not do less than cross over to speak to her. She belonged to a cottage I had left some distance behind, and had been to the farm with a message and was on her way back, she told me, speaking with slow deliberation and profound respect, as to a being of a higher order than man. Then she took my little gift and after making a second careful curtsey proceeded slowly and gravely on her way.

Undoubtedly all this unsmiling, deeply respectful manner was a mask, or we may go so far as to call it second nature, and was the result of living in a cottage in an agricultural district with adults or old people:—probably her grandmother was the poor little darling's model, and any big important-looking man she met was the lord of the manor!

What an amazing difference outwardly between the rustic and the city child of a society woman, accustomed to be addressed and joked with and caressed by scores of persons every day—her own people, friends, visitors, strangers! Such a child I met last summer at a west-end shop or emporium where women congregate in a colossal tea-room under a glass dome, with glass doors opening upon an acre of flat roof.

There, one afternoon, after drinking my tea I walked away to a good distance on the roof and sat down to smoke a cigarette, and presently saw a charming-looking child come dancing out from among the tea-drinkers. Round and round she whirled, heedless of the presence of all those people, happy and free and wild as a lamb running a race with itself on some green flowery down under the wide sky. And by-and-by she came near and was pirouetting round my chair, when I spoke to her, and congratulated her on having had a nice holiday at the seaside. One knew it from her bare brown legs. Oh yes, she said, it was a nice holiday at Bognor, and she had enjoyed it very much.

"Particularly the paddling," I remarked.

No, there was no paddling—her mother wouldn't let her paddle.

"What a cruel mother!" I said, and she laughed merrily, and we talked a little longer, and then seeing her about to go, I said, "you must be just seven years old."

"No, only five," she replied.

"Then," said I, "you must be a wonderfully clever child."

"Oh yes, I know I'm clever," she returned quite naturally, and away she went, spinning over the wide space, and was presently lost in the crowd.

A few minutes later a pleasant-looking but dignified lady came out from among the tea-drinkers and bore down directly on me. "I hear," she said, "you've been talking to my little girl, and I want you to know I was very sorry I couldn't let her paddle. She was just recovering from whooping-cough when I took her to the seaside, and I was afraid to let her go in the water."

I commended her for her prudence, and apologised for having called her cruel, and after a few remarks about her charming child, she went her way.

And now I have no sooner done with this little girl than another cometh up as a flower in my memory and I find I'm compelled to break off. There are too many for me. It is true that the child's beautiful life is a brief one, like that of the angel-insect, and may be told in a paragraph; yet if I were to write only as many of them as there are "Lives" in Plutarch it would still take an entire book—an octavo of at least three hundred pages. But though I can't write the book I shall not leave the subject just yet, and so will make a pause here, to continue the subject in the next sketch, then the next to follow, and probably the next after that.

XVII

MILLICENT AND ANOTHER

They were two quite small maidies, aged respectively four and six years with some odd months in each case. They are older now and have probably forgotten the stranger to whom they gave their fresh little hearts, who presently left their country never to return; for all this happened a long time ago—I think about three years. In a way they were rivals, yet had never seen one another, perhaps never will, since they inhabit two villages more than a dozen miles apart in a wild, desolate, hilly district of West Cornwall.

Let me first speak of Millicent, the elder. I knew Millicent well, having at various times spent several weeks with her in her parents' house, and she, an only child, was naturally regarded as the most important person in it. In Cornwall it is always so. Tall for her years, straight and slim, with no red colour on her cheeks; she had brown hair and large serious grey eyes; those eyes and her general air of gravity, and her forehead, which was too broad for perfect beauty, made me a little shy of her and we were not too intimate. And, indeed, that feeling on my part, which made me a little careful and ceremonious in our intercourse, seemed to be only what she expected of me. One day in a forgetful or expansive moment I happened to call her "Millie," which caused her to look to me in surprise. "Don't you like me to call you Millie—for short?" I questioned apologetically. "No," she returned gravely; "it is not my name—my name is Millicent." And so it had to be to the end of the chapter.

Then there was her speech—I wondered how she got it! For it was unlike that of the people she lived among of her own class. No word-clipping and slurring, no "naughty English" as old Nordin called it, and sing-song intonation with her! She spoke with an almost startling distinctness, giving every syllable its proper value, and her words were as if they had been read out of a nicely written book.

Nevertheless, we got on fairly well together, meeting on most days at tea-time in the kitchen, when we would have nice sober little talks and look at her lessons and books and pictures, sometimes unbending so far as to draw pigs on her slate with our eyes shut, and laughing at the result just like ordinary persons.

It was during my last visit, after an absence of some months from that part of the country, that one evening on coming in I was told by her mother that Millicent had gone for the milk, and that I would have to wait for my tea till she came back. Now the farm that supplied the milk was away at the other end of the village, quite half a mile, and I went to meet her, but did not see her until I had walked the whole distance, when just as I arrived at the gate she came out of the farm-house burdened with a basket of things in one hand and a can of milk in the other. She graciously allowed me to relieve her of both, and taking basket and can with one hand I gave her the other, and so, hand in hand, very friendly, we set off down the long, bleak, windy road just when it was growing dark.

"I'm afraid you are rather thinly clad for this bleak December evening," I remarked. "Your little hand feels cold as ice."

She smiled sweetly and said she was not feeling cold, after which there was a long interval of silence. From time to time we met a villager, a fisherman in his ponderous sea-boots, or a farm-labourer homeward plodding his weary way. But though heavy-footed after his day's labour he is never so stolid as an English ploughman is apt to be; invariably when giving us a good-night in passing the man would smile and look at Millicent very directly with a meaning twinkle in his Cornish eye. He might have been congratulating her on having a male companion to pay her all these nice little attentions, and perhaps signalling the hope that something would come of it.

Grave little Millicent, I was pleased to observe, took no notice of this Cornubian foolishness. At length when we had walked half the distance home, in perfect silence, she said impressively: "Mr. Hudson, I have something I want to tell you very much."

I begged her to speak, pressing her cold little hand.

She proceeded: "I shall never forget that morning when you went away the last time. You said you were going to Truro; but I'm not sure—perhaps it was to London. I only know that it was very far away, and you were going for a very long time. It was early in the morning, and I was in bed. You know how late I always am. I heard you calling to me to come down and say good-bye; so I jumped up and came down in my nightdress and saw you standing waiting for me at the foot of the stairs. Then, when I got down, you took me up in your arms and kissed me. I shall never forget it!"

"Why?" I said, rather lamely, just because it was necessary to say something. And after a little pause, she returned, "Because I shall never forget it."

Then, as I said nothing, she resumed: "That day after school I saw Uncle Charlie and told him, and he said: 'What! you allowed that tramp to kiss you! then I don't want to take you on my knee any more—you've lowered yourself too much.'"

"Did he dare to say that?" I returned.

"Yes, that's what Uncle Charlie said, but it makes no difference. I told him you were not a tramp, Mr. Hudson, and he said you could call yourself Mister-what-you-liked but you were a tramp all the same, nothing but a common tramp, and that I ought to be ashamed of myself. 'You've disgraced the family,' that's what he said, but I don't care—I shall never forget it, the morning you went away and took me up in your arms and kissed me."

Here was a revelation! It saddened me, and I made no reply although I think she expected one. And so after a minute or two of uncomfortable silence she repeated that she would never forget it. For all the time I was thinking of another and sweeter one who was also a person of importance in her own home and village over a dozen miles away.

In thoughtful silence we finished our talk; then there were lights and tea and general conversation; and if Millicent had intended returning to the subject she found no opportunity then or afterwards.

It was better so, seeing that the other character possessed my whole heart. *She* was not intellectual; no one would have said of her, for example, that she would one day blossom into a second Emily Bronte; that to future generations her wild moorland village would be the Haworth of the West. She was perhaps something better—a child of earth and sun, exquisite, with her flossy hair a shining chestnut gold, her eyes like the bugloss, her whole face like a flower or rather like a ripe peach in bloom and colour; we are apt to associate these delicious little beings with flavours as well as fragrances. But I am not going to be so foolish as to attempt to describe her.

Our first meeting was at the village spring, where the women came with pails and pitchers for water; she came, and sitting on the stone rim of the basin into which the water gushed, regarded me smilingly, with questioning eyes. I started a conversation, but though smiling she was shy. Luckily I had my luncheon, which consisted of fruit, in my satchel, and telling her about it she grew interested and confessed to me that of all good things fruit was what she loved best. I then opened my stores, and selecting the brightest yellow and richest purple fruits, told her that they were for her—on one condition—that she would love me and give me a kiss. And she consented and came to me. O that kiss! And what more can I find to say of it? Why nothing, unless one of the poets, Crawshaw for preference, can tell me. "My song," I might say with that mystic, after an angel had kissed him in the morning,

Tasted of that breakfast all day long.

From that time we got on swimmingly, and were much in company, for soon, just to be near her, I went to stay at her village. I then made the discovery that Mab, for that is what they called her, although so unlike, so much softer and sweeter than Millicent, was yet like her in being a child of character and of an indomitable will. She never cried, never argued, or listened to arguments, never demonstrated after the fashion of wilful children generally, by throwing herself down screaming and kicking; she simply very gently insisted on having her own way and living her own life. In the end she always got it, and the beautiful thing was that she never wanted to be naughty or do anything really wrong! She took a quite wonderful interest in the life of the little community, and would always be where others were, especially when any gathering took place. Thus, long before I knew her at the age of four, she made the discovery that the village children, or most of them, passed much of their time in school, and to school she accordingly resolved to go. Her parents opposed, and talked seriously to her and used force to restrain her, but she overcame them in the end, and to the school they had to take her, where she was refused admission on account of her tender years. But she had resolved to go, and go she would; she laid siege to the schoolmistress, to the vicar, who told me how day after day she would come to the door of the vicarage, and the parlour-maid would come rushing into his study to announce, "Miss Mab to speak to you Sir," and how he would talk seriously to her, and then tell her to run home to her mother and be a good child. But it was all in vain, and in the end, because of her importunity or sweetness, he had to admit her.

When I went, during school hours, to give a talk to the children, there I found Mab, one of the forty, sitting with her book, which told her nothing, in her little hands. She listened to the talk with an appearance of interest, although understanding nothing, her bugloss eyes on me, encouraging me with a very sweet smile, whenever I looked her way.

It was the same about attending church. Her parents went to one service on Sundays; she insisted on going to all three, and would sit and stand and kneel, book in hand, as if taking a part in it all, but always when you looked at her, her eyes would meet yours and the sweet smile would come to her lips.

I had been told by her mother that Mab would not have dolls and toys, and this fact, recalled at an opportune moment, revealed to me her secret mind—her baby philosophy. We, the inhabitants of the village, grown-ups and children as well as the domestic animals, were her playmates and playthings, so that she was independent of sham blue-eyed babies made of sawdust and cotton and inanimate fluffy Teddy-bears; she was in possession of the real thing! The cottages, streets, the church and school, the fields and rocks and hills and sea and sky were all contained in her nursery or playground; and we, her fellow-beings, were all occupied from morn to night in an endless complicated game, which varied from day to day according to the weather and time of year, and had many beautiful surprises. She didn't understand it all, but was determined to be in it and get all the fun she could out of it. This mental attitude came out strikingly one day when we had a funeral—always a feast to the villagers; that is to say, an emotional feast; and on this occasion the circumstances made the ceremony a peculiarly impressive one.

A young man, well known and generally liked, son of a small farmer, died with tragic suddenness, and the little stone farm-house being situated away on the borders of the parish, the funeral procession had a considerable distance to walk to the village. To the church I went to view its approach; built on a rock, the church stands high in the centre of the village, and from the broad stone steps in front one got a fine view of the inland country and of the procession like an immense black serpent winding along over green fields and stiles, now disappearing in some hollow ground or behind grey masses of rock, then emerging on the sight, and the voices of the singers bursting out loud and clear in that still atmosphere.

When I arrived on the steps Mab was already there; the whole village would be at that spot presently, but she was first. On that morning no sooner had she heard that the funeral was going to take place than she gave herself a holiday from school and made her docile mother dress her in her daintiest clothes. She welcomed me with a glad face and put her wee hand in mine; then the villagers—all those not in the procession—began to arrive, and very soon we were in the middle of a throng; then, as the six coffin-bearers came slowly toiling up the many steps, and the singing all at once grew loud and swept as a big wave of sound over us, the people were shaken with emotion, and all the faces, even of the oldest men, were wet with tears—all except ours, Mab's and mine.

Our tearless condition—our ability to keep dry when it was raining, so to say—resulted from quite different causes. Mine just then were the eyes of a naturalist curiously observing the demeanour of the beings around me. To Mab the whole spectacle was an act, an interlude, or scene in that wonderful endless play which was a perpetual delight to witness and in which she too was taking a part. And to see all her friends, her grown-up playmates, enjoying themselves in this unusual way, marching in a procession to the church, dressed in black, singing hymns with tears in their eyes—why, this was even better than school or Sunday service, romps in the playground or a children's tea. Every time I looked down at my little mate she lifted a rosy face to mine with her sweetest smile and bugloss eyes aglow with ineffable happiness. And now that we are far apart my loveliest memory of her is as she appeared then. I would not spoil that lovely image by going back to look at her again. Three years! It was said of Lewis Carroll that he ceased to care anything about his little Alices when they had come to the age of ten. Seven is my limit: they are perfect then: but in Mab's case the peculiar exquisite charm could hardly have lasted beyond the age of six.

XVIII

FRECKLES

My meeting with Freckles only served to confirm me in the belief, almost amounting to a conviction, that the female of our species reaches its full mental development at an extraordinarily early age compared to that of the male. In the male the receptive and elastic or progressive period varies greatly; but judging from the number of cases one meets with of men who have continued gaining in intellectual power to the end of their lives, in spite of physical decay, it is reasonable to conclude that the stationary individuals are only so because of the condition of their lives having been inimical. In fact, stagnation strikes us as an unnatural condition of mind. The man who dies at fifty or sixty or seventy, after progressing all his life, doubtless would, if he had lived a lustrum or a decade longer, have attained to a still greater height. "How disgusting it is," cried Ruskin, when he had reached his threescore years and ten, "to find that just when one's getting interested in life one has got to die!" Many can say as much; all could say it, had not the mental machinery been disorganised by some accident, or become rusted from neglect and carelessness. He who is no more in mind at sixty than at thirty is but a half-grown man: his is a case of arrested development.

It is hardly necessary to remark here that the mere accumulation of knowledge is not the same thing as power of mind and its increase: the man who astonishes you with the amount of knowledge stored in his brain may be no greater in mind at seventy than at twenty.

Comparing the sexes again, we might say that the female mind reaches perfection in childhood, long before the physical change from a generalised to a specialised form; whereas the male retains a generalised form to the end of life and never ceases to advance mentally. The reason is obvious. There is no need for continued progression in women, and Nature, like the grand old economist she is, or can be when she likes, matures the mind quickly in one case and slowly in the other; so slowly that he, the young male, goes crawling on all fours as it were, a long distance after his little flying sister—slowly because he has very far to go and must keep on for a very, very long time.

I met Freckles in one of those small ancient out-of-the-world market towns of the West of England—Somerset to be precise—which are just like large old villages, where the turnpike road is for half a mile or so a High Street, wide at one point, where the market is held. For a short distance there are shops on either side, succeeded by quiet dignified houses set back among trees, then by thatched cottages, after which succeed fields and woods.

I had lunched at the large old inn at noon on a hot summer's day; when I sat down a black cloud was coming up, and by-and-by there was thunder, and when I went to the door it was raining heavily. I leant against the frame of the door, sheltered from the wet by a small tiled portico over my head, to wait for the storm to pass before getting on my bicycle. Then the innkeeper's child, aged five, came out and placed herself against the door-frame on the other side. We regarded one another with a good deal of curiosity, for she was a queer-looking little thing. Her head, big for her size and years, was as perfectly round as a Dutch cheese, and her face so thickly freckled that it was all freckles; she had confluent freckles, and as the spots and blotches were of different shades, one could see that they overlapped like the scales of a fish. Her head was bound tightly round with a piece of white calico, and no hair appeared under it.

Just to open the conversation, I remarked that she was a little girl rich in freckles.

"Yes, I know," she returned, "there's no one in the town with such a freckled face."

"And that isn't all," I went on. "Why is your head in a night-cap or a white cloth as if you wanted to hide your hair? or haven't you got any?"

"I can tell you about that," she returned, not in the least resenting my personal remarks. "It is because I've had ringworms. My head is shaved and I'm not allowed to go to school."

"Well," I said, "all these unpleasant experiences—ringworm, shaved head, freckles, and expulsion from school as an undesirable person—do not appear to have depressed you much. You appear quite happy."

She laughed good-humouredly, then looked up out of her blue eyes as if asking what more I had to say.

Just then a small girl about thirteen years old passed us—a child with a thin anxious face burnt by the sun to a dark brown, and deep-set, dark blue, penetrating eyes. It was a face to startle one; and as she went by she stared intently at the little freckled girl.

Then I, to keep the talk going, said I could guess the sort of life that child led.

"What sort of life does she lead?" asked Freckles.

She was, I said, a child from some small farm in the neighbourhood, and had a very hard life, and was obliged to do a great deal more work indoors and out than was quite good for her at her tender age. "But I wonder why she stared at you?" I concluded.

"Did she stare at me!—Why did she stare?"

"I suppose it was because she saw you, a mite of a child, with a nightcap on her head, standing here at the door of the inn talking to a stranger just like some old woman."

She laughed again, and said it was funny for a child of five to be called an old woman. Then, with a sudden change to gravity, she assured me that I had been quite right in what I had said about that little girl. She lived with her parents on a small farm, where no maid was kept, and the little girl did as much work or more than any maid. She had to take the cows to pasture and bring them back; she worked in the fields and helped in the cooking and washing, and came every day to the town with a basket of butter, and eggs, which she had to deliver at a number of houses. Sometimes she came twice in a day, usually in a pony-cart, but when the pony was wanted by her father she had to come on foot with the basket, and the farm was three miles out. On Sunday she didn't come, but had a good deal to do at home.

"Ah, poor little slave! No wonder she gazed at you as she did;—she was thinking how sweet your life must be with people to love and care for you and no hard work to do."

"And was that what made her stare at me, and not because I had a nightcap on and was like an old woman talking to a stranger?" This without a smile.

"No doubt. But you seem to know a great deal about her. Now I wonder if you can tell me something about this beautiful young lady with an umbrella coming towards us? I should much like to know who she is—and I should like to call on her."

"Yes, I can tell you all about her. She is Miss Eva Langton, and lives at the White House. You follow the street till you get out of the town where there is a pond at this end of the common, and just a little the other side of the pond there are big trees, and behind the trees a white gate. That's the gate of the White House, only you can't see it because the trees are in the way. Are you going to call on her?"

I explained that I did not know her, and though I wished I did because she was so pretty, it would not perhaps be quite right to go to her house to see her.

"I'm sorry you're not going to call, she's such a nice young lady. Everybody likes her." And then, after a few moments, she looked up with a smile, and said, "Is there anything else I can tell you about the people of the town? There's a man going by in the rain with a lot of planks on his head—would you like to know who he is and all about him?"

"Oh yes, certainly," I replied. "But of course I don't care so much about him as I do about that little brown girl from the farm, and the nice Miss Langton from the White House. But it's really very pleasant to listen to you whatever you talk about. I really think you one of the most charming little girls I have ever met, and I wonder what you will be like in another five years. I think I must come and see for myself."

"Oh, will you come back in five years? Just to see me! My hair will be grown then and I won't have a nightcap on, and I'll try to wash off the freckles before you come."

"No, don't," I said. "I had forgotten all about them—I think they are very nice."

She laughed, then looking up a little archly, said: "You are saying all that just for fun, are you not?"

"Oh no, nothing of the sort. Just look at me, and say if you do not believe what I tell you."

"Yes, I do," she answered frankly enough, looking full in my eyes with a great seriousness in her own.

That sudden seriousness and steady gaze; that simple, frank declaration! Would five years leave her in that stage? I fancy not, for at ten she would be self-conscious, and the loss would be greater than the gain. No, I would not come back in five years to see what she was like.

That was the end of our talk. She looked towards the wet street and her face changed, and with a glad cry she darted out. The rain was over, and a big man in a grey tweed coat was coming across the road to our side. She met him halfway, and bending down he picked her up and set her on his shoulder and marched with her into the house.

There were others, it seemed, who were able to appreciate her bright mind and could forget all about her freckles and her nightcap.

XIX

ON CROMER BEACH

It is true that when little girls become self-conscious they lose their charm, or the best part of it; they are at their best as a rule from five to seven, after which begins a slow, almost imperceptible decline (or evolution, if you like) until the change is complete. The charm in decline was not good enough for Lewis Carroll; the successive little favourites, we learn, were always dropped at about ten. That was the limit. Perhaps he perceived, with a rare kind of spiritual sagacity resembling that of certain animals with regard to approaching weather-changes, that something had come into their heart, or would shortly come, which would make them no longer precious to him. But that which had made them precious was not far to seek: he would find it elsewhere, and could afford to dismiss his Alice for the time being from his heart and life, and even from his memory, without a qualm.

To my seven-years' rule there are, however, many exceptions—little girls who keep the child's charm in spite of the changes which years and a newly developing sense can bring to them. I have met with some rare instances of the child being as much to us at ten as at five.

One instance which I have in my mind just now is of a little girl of nine, or perhaps nearly ten, and it seemed to me in this case that this new sense, the very quality which is the spoiler of the child-charm, may sometimes have the effect of enhancing it or revealing it in a new and more beautiful aspect.

I met her at Cromer, where she was one of a small group of five visitors; three ladies, one old, the others middle-aged, and a middle-aged gentleman. He and one of the two younger ladies were perhaps her parents, and the elderly lady her grandmother. What and who these people were I never heard, nor did I enquire; but the child attracted me, and in a funny way we became acquainted, and though we never exchanged more than a dozen words, I felt that we were quite intimate and very dear friends.

The little group of grown-ups and the child were always together on the front, where I was accustomed to see them sitting or slowly walking up and down, always deep in conversation and very serious, always regarding the more or less gaudily attired females on the parade with an expression of repulsion. They were old-fashioned in dress and appearance, invariably in black—black silk and black broadcloth. I concluded that they were serious people, that they had inherited and faithfully kept a religion, or religious temper, which has long been outlived by the world in general—a puritanism or Evangelicalism dating back to the far days of Wilberforce and Hannah More and the ancient Sacred order of Claphamites.

And the child was serious with them and kept pace with them with slow staid steps. But she was beautiful, and under the mask and mantle which had been imposed on her had a shining child's soul. Her large eyes were blue, the rare blue of a perfect summer's day. There was no need to ask her where she had got that colour; undoubtedly in heaven "as she came through." The features were perfect, and she pale, or so it had seemed to me at first, but when viewing her more closely I saw that colour was an important element in her loveliness—a colour so delicate that I fell to comparing her flower-like face with this or that particular flower. I had thought of her as a snowdrop at first, then a windflower, the March anemone, with its touch of crimson, then various white, ivory, and cream-coloured blossoms with a faintly-seen pink blush to them.

Her dress, except the stocking, was not black; it was grey or dove-colour, and over it a cream or pale-fawn-coloured cloak with hood, which with its lace border seemed just the right setting for the delicate puritan face. She walked in silence while they talked and talked, ever in grave subdued tones. Indeed it would not have been seemly for her to open her lips in such company. I called her Priscilla, but she was also like Milton's pensive nun, devout and pure, only her looks were not commercing with the skies; they were generally cast down, although it is probable that they did occasionally venture to glance at the groups of merry pink-legged children romping with the waves below.

I had seen her three or four or more times on the front before we became acquainted; and she too had noticed me, just raising her blue eyes to mine when we passed one another, with a shy sweet look of recognition in them—a questioning look; so that we were not exactly strangers. Then, one morning, I sat on the front when the black-clothed group came by, deep in serious talk as usual, the silent child with them, and after a turn or two they sat down beside me. The tide was at its full and children were coming down to their old joyous pastime of paddling. They were a merry company. After watching them I glanced at my little neighbour and caught her eyes, and she knew what the question in my mind was—Why are not you with them? And she was pleased and troubled at the same time, and her face was all at once in a glow of beautiful colour; it was the colour of the almond blossom;—her sister flower on this occasion.

A day or two later we were more fortunate. I went before breakfast to the beach and was surprised to find her there watching the tide coming in; in a moment of extreme indulgence her mother, or her people, had allowed her to run down to look at the sea for a minute by herself. She was standing on the shingle, watching the green waves break frothily at her feet, her pale face transfigured with a gladness which seemed almost unearthly. Even then in that emotional moment the face kept its tender flower-like character; I could only compare it to the sweet-pea blossom, ivory white or delicate pink; that Psyche-like flower with wings upraised to fly, and expression of infantile innocence and fairy-like joy in life.

I walked down to her and we then exchanged our few and only words. How beautiful the sea was, and how delightful to watch the waves coming in! I remarked. She smiled and replied that it was very, very beautiful. Then a bigger wave came and compelled us to step hurriedly back to save our feet from a wetting, and we laughed together. Just at that spot there was a small rock on which I stepped and asked her to give me her hand, so that we could stand together and let the next wave rush by without wetting us. "Oh, do you think I may?" she said, almost frightened at such an adventure. Then, after a moment's hesitation, she put her hand in mine, and we stood on the little fragment of rock, and she watched the water rush up and surround us and break on the beach with a fearful joy. And after that wonderful experience she had to leave me; she had only been allowed out by herself for five minutes, she said, and so, after a grateful smile, she hurried back.

Our next encounter was on the parade, where she appeared as usual with her people, and nothing beyond one swift glance of recognition and greeting could pass between us. But it was a quite wonderful glance she gave me, it said so much:—that we had a great secret between us and were friends and comrades for ever. It would take half a page to tell all that was conveyed in that glance. "I'm so glad to see you," it said, "I was beginning to fear you had gone away. And now how unfortunate that you see me with my people and we cannot speak! They wouldn't understand. How could they, since they don't belong to our world and know what we know? If I were to explain that we are different from them, that we want to play together on the beach and watch the waves and paddle and build castles, they would say, 'Oh yes, that's all very well, but—' I shouldn't know what they meant by that, should you? I do hope we'll meet again some day and stand once more hand in hand on the beach—don't you?"

And with that she passed on and was gone, and I saw her no more. Perhaps that glance which said so much had been observed, and she had been hurriedly removed to some place of safety at a great distance. But though I never saw her again, never again stood hand in hand with her on the beach and never shall, I have her picture to keep in all its flowery freshness and beauty, the most delicate and lovely perhaps of all the pictures I possess of the little girls I have met.

XX

DIMPLES

It is not pleasant when you have had your say, made your point to your own satisfaction, and gone cheerfully on to some fresh subject, to be assailed with the suspicion that your interlocutor is saying mentally: All very well—very pretty talk, no doubt, but you haven't convinced me, and I even doubt that you have succeeded in convincing yourself!

For example, a reader of the foregoing notes may say: "If you really find all this beauty and charm and fascination you tell us in some little girls, you must love them. You can't admire and take delight in them as you can in a piece of furniture, or tapestry, or a picture or statue or a stone of great brilliancy and purity of colour, or in any beautiful inanimate object, without that emotion coming in to make itself part of and one with your admiration. You can't, simply because a child is a human being, and we do not want to lose sight of the being we love. So long as the love lasts, the eye would follow its steps because—we are what we are, and a mere image in the mind doesn't satisfy the heart. Love is never satisfied, and asks not for less and less each day but for more—always for more. Then, too, love is credulous; it believes and imagines all things and, like all emotions, it pushes reason and experience aside and sticks to the belief that these beautiful qualities cannot die and leave nothing behind: they are not on the surface only; they have their sweet permanent roots in the very heart and centre of being."

That, I suppose, is the best argument on the other side, and if you look straight at it for six seconds, you will see it dissolve like a lump of sugar in a tumbler of water and disappear under your very eyes. For the fact remains that when I listen to the receding footsteps of my little charmer, the sigh that escapes me expresses something of relief as well as regret. The signs of change have perhaps not yet appeared, and I wish not to see them. Good-bye, little one, we part in good time, and may we never meet again! Undoubtedly one loses something, but it cannot balance the gain. The loss in any case was bound to come, and had I waited for it no gain would have been possible. As it is, I am like that man in *The Pilgrim's Progress*, by some accounted mad, who the more he cast away the more he had. And the way of it is this; by losing my little charmers before they cease from charming, I make them mine for always, in a sense. They are made mine because my mind (other minds, too) is made that way. That which I see with delight I continue to see when it is no more there, and will go on seeing to the end: at all events I fail to detect any sign of decay or fading in these mind pictures. There are people with money who collect gems—diamonds, rubies and other precious stones—who value their treasures as their best possessions, and take them out from time to time to examine and gloat over them. These things are trash to me compared with the shining, fadeless images in my mind, which are my treasures and best possessions. But the bright and beauteous images of the little girl charmers would not have been mine if instead of letting the originals disappear from my ken I had kept them too long in it. All because our minds, our memories are made like that. If we see a thing once, or several times, we see it ever after as we first saw it; if we go on seeing it every day or every week for years and years, we do not register a countless series of new distinct impressions, recording all its changes: the new impressions fall upon and obliterate the others, and it is like a series of photographs, not arranged side by side for future inspection, but in a pile, the top one alone remaining visible. Looking at this insipid face you would not believe, if told, that once upon a time it was beautiful to you and had a great charm. The early impressions are lost, the charm forgotten.

This reminds me of the incident I set out to narrate when I wrote "Dimples" at the head of this note. I was standing at a busy corner in a Kensington thoroughfare waiting for a bus, when a group of three ladies appeared and came to a stand a yard or two from me and waited, too, for the traffic to pass before attempting to cross to the other side. One was elderly and feeble and was holding the arm of another of the trio, who was young and pretty. Her age was perhaps twenty; she was of medium height, slim, with a nice figure and nicely dressed. She was a blonde, with light blue-grey eyes and fluffy hair of pale gold: there was little colour in her face, but the features were perfect and the mouth with its delicate curves quite beautiful.

But after regarding her attentively for a minute or so, looking out impatiently for my bus at the same time, I said mentally: "Yes, you are certainly very pretty, perhaps beautiful, but I don't like you and I don't want you. There's nothing in you to correspond to that nice outside. You are an exception to the rule that the beautiful is the good. Not that you are bad—actively, deliberately bad—you haven't the strength to be that or anything else; you have only a little shallow mind and a little coldish heart."

Now I can imagine one of my lady readers crying out: "How dared you say such monstrous things of any person after just a glance at her face?"

Listen to me, madam, and you will agree that I was not to blame for saying these monstrous things. All my life I've had the instinct or habit of seeing the things I see; that is to say, seeing them not as cloud or mist-shapes for ever floating past, nor as people in endless procession "seen rather than distinguished," but distinctly, separately, as individuals each with a character and soul of its very own; and while seeing it in that way some little unnamed faculty in some obscure corner of my brain hastily scribbles a label to stick on to the object or person before it passes out of sight. It can't be prevented; it goes on automatically; it isn't *me*, and I can no more interfere or attempt in any way to restrain or regulate its action than I can take my legs to task for running up a flight of steps without the mind's supervision.

But I haven't finished with the young lady yet. I had no sooner said what I have said and was just about to turn my eyes away and forget all about her, when, in response to some remarks of her aged companion, she laughed, and in laughing so great a change came into her face that it was as if she had been transformed into another being. It was like a sudden breath of wind and a sunbeam falling on the still cold surface of a woodland pool. The eyes, icily cold a moment before, had warm sunlight in them, and the half-parted lips with a flash of white teeth between them had gotten a new beauty; and most remarkable of all was a dimple which appeared and in its swift motions seemed to have a life of its own, flitting about the corner of the mouth, then further away to the middle of the cheek and back again. A dimple that had a story to tell. For dimples, too, like a delicate, mobile mouth, and even like eyes, have a character of their own. And no sooner had I seen that sudden change in the expression, and especially the dimple, than I knew the face; it was a face I was familiar with and was like no other face in the world, yet I could not say who she was nor where and when I had known her! Then, when the smile faded and the dimple vanished, she was a stranger again—the pretty young person with the shallow brain that I did not like!

Naturally my mind worried itself with this puzzle of a being with two distinct expressions, one strange to me, the other familiar, and it went on worrying me all that day until I could stand it no longer, and to get rid of the matter, I set up the theory (which didn't quite convince me) that the momentary expression I had seen was like an expression in some one I had known in the far past. But after dismissing the subject in that way, the subconscious mind was still no doubt working at it, for two days later it all at once flashed into my mind that my mysterious young lady was no other than the little Lillian I had known so well eight years before! She was ten years old when I first knew her, and I was quite intimately acquainted with her for a little over a year, and greatly admired her for her beauty and charm, especially when she smiled and that dimple flew about the corner of her mouth like a twilight moth vaguely fluttering at the rim of a red flower. But alas! her charm was waning: she was surrounded by relations who adored her, and was intensely self-conscious, so that when after a year her people moved to a new district, I was not sorry to break the connection, and to forget all about her.

Now that I had seen and remembered her again, it was a consolation to think that she was already in her decline when I first knew and was attracted by her and on that account had never wholly lost my heart to her. How different my feelings would have been if after pronouncing that irrevocable judgment, I had recognised one of my vanished darlings—one, say, like that child on Cromer Beach, or of dozens of other fairylike little ones I have known and loved, and whose images are enduring and sacred!

XXI

WILD FLOWERS AND LITTLE GIRLS

Thinking of the numerous company of little girls of infinite charm I have met, and of their evanishment, I have a vision of myself on horseback on the illimitable green level pampas, under the wide sunlit cerulean sky in late September or early October, when the wild flowers are at their best before the wilting heats of summer.

Seeing the flowers so abundant, I dismount and lead my horse by the bridle and walk knee-deep in the lush grass, stooping down at every step to look closely at the shy, exquisite blooms in their dewy morning freshness and divine colours. Flowers of an inexpressible unearthly loveliness and unforgettable; for how forget them when their images shine in memory in all their pristine morning brilliance!

That is how I remember and love to remember them, in that first fresh aspect, not as they appear later, the petals wilted or dropped, sun-browned, ripening their seed and fruit.

And so with the little human flowers. I love to remember and think of them as flowers, not as ripening or ripened into young ladies, wives, matrons, mothers of sons and daughters.

As little girls, as human flowers, they shone and passed out of sight. Only of one do I think differently, the most exquisite among them, the most beautiful in body and soul, or so I imagine, perhaps because of the manner of her vanishing even while my eyes were still on her. That was Dolly, aged eight, and because her little life finished then she is the one that never faded, never changed.

Here are some lines I wrote when grief at her going was still fresh. They were in a monthly magazine at that time years ago, and were set to music, although not very successfully, and I wish it could be done again.

> Should'st thou come to me again
> From the sunshine and the rain,
> With thy laughter sweet and free,
> O how should I welcome thee!

> Like a streamlet dark and cold
> Kindled into fiery gold
> By a sunbeam swift that cleaves
> Downward through the curtained leaves;

> So this darkened life of mine
> Lit with sudden joy would shine,
> And to greet thee I should start
> With a great cry in my heart.

> Back to drop again, the cry
> On my trembling lips would die:
> Thou would'st pass to be again
> With the sunshine and the rain.

XXII

A LITTLE GIRL LOST

Yet once more, O ye little girls, I come to bid you a last good-bye—a very last one this time. Not to you, living little girls, seeing that I must always keep a fair number of you on my visiting list, but to a fascinating theme I had to write about. For I did really and truly think I had quite finished with it, and now all at once I find myself compelled by a will stronger than my own to make this one further addition. The will of a little girl who is not present and is lost to me—a wordless message from a distance, to tell me that she is not to be left out of this gallery. And no sooner has her message come than I find there are several good reasons why she should be included, the first and obvious one being that she will be a valuable acquisition, an ornament to the said gallery. And here I will give a second reason, a very important one (to the psychological minded at all events), but not the most important of all, for that must be left to the last.

In the foregoing impressions of little girls I have touched on the question of the child's age when that "little agitation in the brain called thought," begins. There were two remarkable cases given; one, the child who climbed upon my knee to amaze and upset me by her pessimistic remarks about life; the second, my little friend Nesta—that was her name and she is still on my visiting list—who revealed her callow mind striving to grasp an abstract idea—the idea of time apart from some visible or tangible object. Now these two were aged five years; but what shall we say of the child, the little girl-child who steps out of the cradle, so to speak, as a being breathing thoughtful breath?

It makes me think of the cradle as the cocoon or chrysalis in which, as by a miracle (for here natural and supernatural seem one and the same), the caterpillar has undergone his transformation and emerging spreads his wings and forthwith takes his flight a full-grown butterfly with all its senses and faculties complete.

Walking on the sea front at Worthing one late afternoon in late November, I sat down at one end of a seat in a shelter, the other end being occupied by a lady in black, and between us, drawn close up to the seat, was a perambulator in which a little girl was seated. She looked at me, as little girls always do, with that question—What are you? in her large grey intelligent eyes. The expression tempted me to address her, and I said I hoped she was quite well.

"O yes," she returned readily. "I am quite well, thank you."

"And may I know how old you are?"

"Yes, I am just three years old."

I should have thought, I said, that as she looked a strong healthy child she would have been able to walk and run about at the age of three.

She replied that she could walk and run as well as any child, and that she had her pram just to sit and rest in when tired of walking.

Then, after apologising for putting so many questions to her, I asked her if she could tell me her name.

"My name," she said, "is Rose Mary Catherine Maude Caversham," or some such name.

"Oh!" exclaimed the lady in black, opening her lips for the first time, and speaking sharply. "You must not say all those names! It is enough to say your name is Rose."

The child turned and looked at her, studying her face, and then with heightened colour and with something like indignation in her tone, she replied: "That *is* my name! Why should I not tell it when I am asked?"

The lady said nothing, and the child turned her face to me again.

I said it was a very pretty name and I had been pleased to hear it, and glad she told it to me without leaving anything out.

Silence still on the part of the lady.

"I think," I resumed, "that you are a rather wonderful child;—have they taught you the ABC?"

"Oh no, they don't teach me things like that—I pick all that up."

"And one and one make two—do you pick that up as well?"

"Yes, I pick that up as well."

"Then," said I, recollecting Humpty Dumpty's question in arithmetic to Alice, "how much is one-an'-one-an'-one-an'-one-an'-one-an'-one?"—speaking it as it should be spoken, very rapidly.

She looked at me quite earnestly for a moment, then said, "And can *you* tell me how much is two-an'-two-an'-two-an'-two-an'-two-an'-two?"—and several more two's all in a rapid strain.

"No," I said, "you have turned the tables on me very cleverly. But tell me, do they teach you nothing?"

"Oh yes, they teach me something!" Then dropping her head a little on one side and lifting her little hands she began practising scales on the bar of her pram. Then, looking at me with a half-smile on her lips, she said: "That's what they teach me."

After a little further conversation she told me she was from London, and was down with her people for their holiday.

I said it seemed strange to me she should be having a holiday so late in the season. "Look," I said, "at that cold grey sea and the great stretch of sand with only one group of two or three children left on it with their little buckets and spades."

"Yes," she said, in a meditative way; "it is very late." Then, after a pause, she turned towards me with an expression in her face which said plainly enough: I am now going to give you a little confidential information. Her words were: "The fact is we are just waiting for the baby."

"Oh!" screamed the lady in black. "Why have you said such a thing! You must not say such things!"

And again the child turned her head and looked earnestly, inquiringly at the lady, trying, as one could see from her face, to understand why she was not to say such a thing. But now she was not sure of her ground as on the other occasion of being rebuked. There was a mystery here about the expected baby which she could not fathom. Why was it wrong for her to mention that simple fact? That question was on her face when she looked at her attendant, the lady in black, and as no answer was forthcoming, either from the lady, or out of her own head, she turned to me again, the dissatisfied expression still in her eyes; then it passed away and she smiled. It was a beautiful smile, all the more because it came only at rare intervals and quickly vanished, because, as it seemed to me, she was all the time thinking too closely about what was being said to smile easily or often. And the rarity of her smile made her sense of humour all the more apparent. She was not like Marjorie Fleming, that immortal little girl, who was wont to be angry when offensively condescending grown-ups addressed her as a babe in intellect. For Marjorie had no real sense of humour; all the humour of her literary composition, verse and prose, was of the unconscious variety. This child was only amused at being taken for a baby.

Then came the parting. I said I had spent a most delightful hour with her, and she, smiling once more put out her tiny hand, and said in the sweetest voice: "Perhaps we shall meet again." Those last five words! If she had been some great lady, an invalid in a bath-chair, who had conversed for half an hour with a perfect stranger and had wished to express the pleasure and interest she had had in the colloquy, she could not have said more, nor less, nor said it more graciously, more beautifully.

But we did not meet again, for when I looked for her she was not there: she had gone out of my life, like Priscilla, and like so many beautiful things that vanish and return not.

And now I return to what I said at the beginning—that there were several reasons for including this little girl in my series of impressions. The most important one has been left until now. I want to meet her again, but how shall I find her in this immensity of London—these six millions of human souls! Let me beg of any reader who knows Rose Mary Angela Catherine Maude Caversham—a name like that—who has identified her from my description—that he will inform me of her whereabouts.

XXIII

A SPRAY OF SOUTHERNWOOD

To pass from little girls to little boys is to go into quite another, an inferior, coarser world. No doubt there are wonderful little boys, but as a rule their wonderfulness consists in a precocious intellect: this kind doesn't appeal to me, so that if I were to say anything on the matter, it would be a prejudiced judgment. Even the ordinary civilised little boy, the nice little gentleman who is as much at home in the drawing-room as at his desk in the school-room or with a bat in the playing-field—even that harmless little person seems somehow unnatural, or denaturalised to my primitive taste. A result, I will have it, of improper treatment. He has been under the tap, too thoroughly scrubbed, boiled, strained and served up with melted butter and a sprig of parsley for ornament in a gilt-edged dish. I prefer him raw, and would rather have the street-Arab, if in town, and the unkempt, rough and tough cottage boy in the country. But take them civilised or natural, those who love and observe little children no more expect to find that peculiar exquisite charm of the girl-child which I have endeavoured to describe in the boy, than they would expect the music of the wood-lark and the airy fairy grace and beauty of the grey wagtail in Philip Sparrow. And yet, incredible as it seems, that very quality of the miraculous little girl is sometimes found in the boy and, with it, strange to say, the boy's proper mind and spirit. The child lover will meet with one of that kind once in ten years, or not so often—not oftener than a collector of butterflies will meet with a Camberwell Beauty. The miraculous little girl, we know, is not more uncommon than the Painted Lady, or White Admiral. And I will here give a picture of such a boy—the child associated in my mind with a spray of southernwood.

And after this impression, I shall try to give one or two of ordinary little boys. These live in memory like the little girls I have written about, not, it will be seen, because of their boy nature, seeing that the boy has nothing miraculous, nothing to capture the mind and register an enduring impression in it, as in the case of the girl; but owing solely to some unusual circumstance in their lives —something adventitious.

It was hot and fatiguing on the Wiltshire Downs, and when I had toiled to the highest point of a big hill where a row of noble Scotch firs stood at the roadside, I was glad to get off my bicycle and rest in the shade. Fifty or sixty yards from the spot where I sat on the bank on a soft carpet of dry grass and pine-needles, there was a small, old, thatched cottage, the only human habitation in sight except the little village at the foot of the hill, just visible among the trees a mile ahead. An old woman in the cottage had doubtless seen me going by, for she now came out into the road, and, shading her eyes with her hand, peered curiously at me. A bent and lean old woman in a dingy black dress, her face brown and wrinkled, her hair white. With her, watching me too, was a little mite of a boy; and after they had stood there a while he left her and went into the cottage garden, but presently came out into the road again and walked slowly towards me. It was strange to see that child in such a place! He had on a scarlet shirt or blouse, wide lace collar, and black knickerbockers and stockings; but it was his face rather than his clothes that caused me to wonder. Rarely had I seen a more beautiful child, such a delicate rose-coloured skin, and fine features, eyes of such pure intense blue, and such shining golden hair. How came this angelic little being in that poor remote cottage with that bent and wrinkled old woman for a guardian?

He walked past me very slowly, a sprig of southernwood in his hand; then after going by he stopped and turned, and approaching me in a shy manner and without saying a word offered me the little pale green feathery spray. I took it and thanked him, and we entered into conversation, when I discovered that his little mind was as bright and beautiful as his little person. He loved the flowers, both garden and wild, but above everything he loved the birds; he watched them to find their nests; there was nothing he liked better than to look at the little spotted eggs in the nest. He could show me a nest if I wanted to see one, only the little bird was sitting on her eggs. He was six years old, and that cottage was his home—he knew no other; and the old bent woman standing there in the road was his mother. They didn't keep a pig, but they kept a yellow cat, only he was lost now; he had gone away, and they didn't know where to find him. He went to school now—he walked all the way there by himself and all the way back every day. It was very hard at first, because the other boys laughed at and plagued him. Then they hit him, but he hit them back as hard as he could. After that they hurt him, but they couldn't make him cry. He never cried, and always hit them back, and now they were beginning to leave him alone. His father was named Mr. Job, and he worked at the farm, but he couldn't do so much work now because he was such an old man. Sometimes when he came home in the evening he sat in his chair and groaned as if it hurt him. And he had two sisters; one was Susan; she was married and had three big girls; and Jane was married too, but had no children. They lived a great way off. So did his brother. His name was Jim, and he was a great fat man and sometimes came from London, where he lived, to see them. He didn't know much about Jim; he was very silent, but not with mother. Those two would shut themselves up together and talk and talk, but no one knew what they were talking about. He would write to mother too; but she would always hide the letters and say to father: "It's only from Jim; he says he's very well—that's all." But they were very long letters, so he must have said more than that.

Thus he prattled, while I, to pay him for the southernwood, drew figures of the birds he knew best on the leaves I tore from my note-book and gave them to him. He thanked me very prettily and put them in his pocket.

"And what is your name?" I asked.

He drew himself up before me and in a clear voice, pronouncing the words in a slow measured manner, as if repeating a lesson, he answered: "Edmund Jasper Donisthorpe Stanley Overington."

The name so astonished me that I remained silent for quite two minutes during which I repeated it to myself many times to fix it in my memory.

"But why," said I at length, "do you call yourself Overington when your father's name is Job?"

"Oh, that is because I have two fathers—Mr. Job, my very old father, and Mr. Overington, who lives away from here. He comes to see me sometimes, and he is my father too; but I have only one mother—there she is out again looking at us."

I questioned him no further, and no further did I seek those mysteries to disclose, and so we parted; but I never see a plant or sprig of southernwood, nor inhale its cedarwood smell, which one does not know whether to like or dislike, without recalling the memory of that miraculous cottage child with a queer history and numerous names.

XXIV

IN PORTCHESTER CHURCHYARD

To the historically and archaeologically minded the castle and walls at Portchester are of great importance. Romans, Britons, Saxons, Normans—they all made use of this well-defended place for long centuries, and it still stands, much of it well preserved, to be explored and admired by many thousands of visitors every year. What most interested me was the sight of two small boys playing in the churchyard. The village church, as at Silchester, is inside the old Roman walls, in a corner, the village itself being some distance away. After strolling round the churchyard I sat down on a stone under the walls and began watching the two boys—little fellows of the cottage class from the village who had come, each with a pair of scissors, to trim the turf on two adjoining mounds. The bigger of the two, who was about ten years old, was very diligent and did his work neatly, trimming the grass evenly and giving the mound a nice smooth appearance. The other boy was not so much absorbed in his work; he kept looking up and making jeering remarks and faces at the other, and at intervals his busy companion put down his shears and went for him with tremendous spirit. Then a chase among and over the graves would begin; finally, they would close, struggle, tumble over a mound and pommel one another with all their might. The struggle over, they would get up, shake off the dust and straws, and go back to their work. After a few minutes the youngest boy recovered from his punishment, and, getting tired of the monotony, would begin teasing again, and a fresh flight and battle would ensue.

By-and-by, after witnessing several of these fights, I went down and sat on a mound next to theirs and entered into conversation with them.

"Whose grave are you trimming?" I asked the elder boy.

It was his sister's, he said, and when I asked him how long she had been dead, he answered, "Twenty years." She had died more than ten years before he was born. He said there had been eight of them born, and he was the youngest of the lot; his eldest brother was married and had children five or six years old. Only one of the eight had died—this sister, when she was a little girl. Her name was Mary, and one day every week his mother sent him to trim the mound. He did not remember when it began—he must have been very small. He had to trim the grass, and in summer to water it so as to keep it always smooth and fresh and green.

Before he had finished his story the other little fellow, who was not interested in it and was getting tired again, began in a low voice to mock at his companion, repeating his words after him. Then my little fellow, with a very serious, resolute air, put the scissors down, and in a moment they were both up and away, doubling this way and that, bounding over the mounds, like two young dogs at play, until, rolling over together, they fought again in the grass. There I left them and strolled away, thinking of the mother busy and cheerful in her cottage over there in the village, but always with that image of the little girl, dead these twenty years, in her heart.

XXV

HOMELESS

One cold morning at Penzance I got into an omnibus at the station to travel to the small town of St. Just, six or seven miles away. Just before we started, a party of eight or ten queer-looking people came hurriedly up and climbed to the top seats. They were men and women, with two or three children, the women carelessly dressed, the men chalky-faced and long-haired, in ulsters of light colours and large patterns. When we had travelled two or three miles one of the outside passengers climbed down and came in to escape from the cold, and edged into a place opposite mine. He was a little boy of about seven or eight years old, and he had a small, quaint face with a tired expression on it, and wore a soiled scarlet Turkish fez on his head, and a big pepper-and-salt overcoat heavily trimmed with old, ragged imitation astrachan. He was keenly alive to the sensation his entrance created among us when the loud buzz of conversation ceased very suddenly and all eyes were fixed on him; but he bore it very bravely, sitting back in his seat, rubbing his cold hands together, then burying them deep in his pockets and fixing his eyes on the roof. Soon the talk recommenced, and the little fellow, wishing to feel more free, took his hands out and tried to unbutton his coat. The top button—a big horn button—resisted the efforts he made with his stiff little fingers, so I undid it for him and threw the coat open, disclosing a blue jersey striped with red, green velvet knickerbockers, and black stockings, all soiled like the old scarlet flower-pot shaped cap. In his get-up he reminded me of a famous music-master and composer of my acquaintance, whose sense of harmony is very perfect with regard to sounds, but exceedingly crude as to colours. Imagine a big, long-haired man arrayed in a bottle-green coat, scarlet waistcoat, pink necktie, blue trousers, white hat, purple gloves and yellow boots! If it were not for the fact that he wears his clothes a very long time and never has them brushed or the grease spots taken out, the effect would be almost painful. But he selects his colours, whereas the poor little boy probably had no choice in the matter.

By-and-by the humorous gentlemen who sat on either side of him began to play him little tricks, one snatching off his scarlet cap and the other blowing on his neck. He laughed a little, just to show that he didn't object to a bit of fun at his expense, but when the annoyance was continued he put on a serious face, and folding up his cap thrust it into his overcoat pocket. He was not going to be made a butt of!

"Where is your home?" I asked him.

"I haven't got a home," he returned.

"What, no home? Where was your home when you had one?"

"I never had a home," he said. "I've always been travelling; but sometimes we stay a month in a place." Then, after an interval, he added: "I belong to a dramatic company."

"And do you ever go on the stage to act?" I asked.

"Yes," he returned, with a weary little sigh.

Then our journey came to an end, and we saw the doors and windows of the St. Just Working Men's Institute aflame with yellow placards announcing a series of sensational plays to be performed there.

The queer-looking people came down and straggled off to the Institute, paying no attention to the small boy. "Let me advise you," I said, standing over him on the pavement, "to treat yourself to a stiff tumbler of grog after your cold ride," and at the same time I put my hand in my pocket.

He didn't smile, but at once held out his open hand. I put some pence in it, and clutching them he murmured "Thank you," and went after the others.

XXVI

THE STORY OF A SKULL

A quarter of a century ago there were still to be seen in the outer suburbs of London many good old roomy houses, standing in their own ample and occasionally park-like grounds, which have now ceased to exist. They were old manor-houses, mostly of the Georgian period, some earlier, and some, too, were fine large farmhouses which a century or more ago had been turned into private residences of city merchants and other persons of means. Any middle-aged Londoner can recall a house or perhaps several houses of this description, and in one of those that were best known to me I met with the skull, the story of which I wish to tell.

It was a very old-looking, long, low red-brick building, with a verandah in front, and being well within the grounds, sheltered by old oak, elm, ash and beech trees, could hardly be seen from the road. The lawns and gardens were large, and behind them were two good-sized grass fields. Within the domain one had the feeling that he was far away in the country in one of its haunts of ancient peace, and yet all round it, outside of its old hedges and rows of elms, the ground had been built over, mostly with good-sized brick houses standing in their own gardens. It was a favourite suburb with well-to-do persons in the city, rents were high and the builders had long been coveting and trying to get possession of all this land which was "doing no good," in a district where haunts of ancients peace were distinctly out of place and not wanted. But the owner (aged ninety-eight) refused to sell.

Not only the builders, but his own sons and sons' sons had represented to him that the rent he was getting for this property was nothing but an old song compared to what it would bring in, if he would let it on a long building lease. There was room there for thirty or forty good houses with big gardens. And his answer invariably was: "It shan't be touched! I was born in that house, and though I'm too old ever to go and see it again, it must not be pulled down—not a brick of it, not a tree cut, while I'm alive. When I'm gone you can do what you like, because then I shan't know what you are doing."

My friends and relations, who were in occupation of the house, and loved it, hoped that he would go on living many, many years: but alas! the visit of the feared dark angel was to them and not to the old owner, who was perhaps "too old to die"; the dear lady of the house and its head was taken away and the family broken up, and from that day to this I have never ventured to revisit that sweet spot, nor sought to know what has been done to it.

At that time it used to be my week-end home, and on one of my early visits I noticed the skull of an animal nailed to the wall about a yard above the stable door. It was too high to be properly seen without getting a ladder, and when the gardener told me that it was a bulldog's skull, I thought no more about it.

One day, several months later, I took a long look at it and got the idea that it was not a bulldog's skull—that it was more like the skull of a human being of a very low type. I then asked my hostess to let me have it, and she said, "Yes, certainly, take it if you want it." Then she added, "But what in the world do you want that horrid old skull for?" I said I wanted to find out what it was, and then she told me that it was a bulldog's skull—the gardener had told her. I replied that I did not think so, that it looked to me more like the skull of a cave-man who had inhabited those parts half a million years ago, perhaps. This speech troubled her very much, for she was a religious woman, and it pained her to hear unorthodox statements about the age of man on the earth. She said that I could not have the skull, that it was dreadful to her to hear me say it might be a human skull; that she would order the gardener to take it down and bury it somewhere in the grounds at a distance from the house. Until that was done she would not go near the stables—it would be like a nightmare to see that dreadful head on the wall. I said I would remove it immediately; it was mine, as she had given it to me, and it was not a man's skull at all—I was only joking, so that she need not have any qualms about it.

That pacified her, and I took down the old skull, which looked more dreadful than ever when I climbed up to it, for though the dome of it was bleached white, the huge eye cavities and mouth were black and filled with old black mould and dead moss. Doubtless it had been very many years in that place, as the long nails used in fastening it there were eaten up with rust.

When I got back to London the box with the skull in it was put away in my book-room, and rested there forgotten for two or three years. Then one day I was talking on natural history subjects to my publisher, and he told me that his son, just returned from Oxford, had developed a keen interest in osteology and was making a collection of mammalian skulls from the whale and elephant and hippopotamus to the harvest-mouse and lesser shrew. This reminded me of the long-forgotten skull, and I told him I had something to send him for his boy's collection, but before sending it I would find out what it was. Accordingly I sent the skull to Mr. Frank E. Beddard, the prosector of the Zoological Society, asking him to tell me what it was. His reply was that it was the skull of an adult gorilla—a fine large specimen.

It was then sent on to the young collector of skulls—who will, alas! collect no more, having now given his life to his country. It saddened me a little to part with it, certainly not because it was a pretty object to possess, but only because that bleached dome beneath which brains were once housed, and those huge black cavities which were once the windows of a strange soul, and that mouth that once had a fleshy tongue that youled and clicked in an unknown language could not tell me its own life-and-death history from the time of its birth in the African forest to its final translation to a wall over a stable door in an old house near London.

There are now several writers on animals who are not exactly naturalists, nor yet mere fictionists, but who, to a considerable knowledge of animal psychology and extraordinary sympathy with all wildness, unite an imaginative insight which reveals to them much of the inner, the mind life of brutes. No doubt the greatest of these is Charles Roberts, the Canadian, and I only wish it had been he who had discovered the old gorilla skull above the stable door, and that the incident had fired the creative brain which gave us *Red Fox* and many another wonderful biography.

Now here is an odd coincidence. After writing the skull story it came into my head to relate it to a lady I was dining with, and I also told her of my intention of putting it in this book of Little Things. She said it was funny that she too had a story of a skull which she had thought of telling in her volume of Little Things; but no, she would not venture to do so, although it was a better story than mine.

She was good enough to let me hear it, and as it is not to appear elsewhere I can't resist the temptation of bringing it in here.

On her return to Europe after travelling and residing for some years in the Far East, she established herself in Paris and proceeded to decorate her apartment with some of the wonderful rich and rare objects she had collected in outlandish parts. Gorgeous fabrics, embroideries, pottery, metal and woodwork, and along with these products of an ancient civilisation, others of rude or primitive tribes, quaint headgear and plumes, strings and ropes of beads, worn as garments by people who run wild in woods, with arrows, spears and other weapons. These last were arranged in the form of a wheel over the entrance, with the bleached and polished skull of an orang-utan in the centre. It was a very perfect skull, with all the formidable teeth intact and highly effective.

She lived happily for some months in her apartment and was very popular in Parisian society and visited by many distinguished people, who all greatly admired her Eastern decorations, especially the skull, before which they would stand expressing their delight with fervent exclamations.

One day when on a visit at a friend's house, her host brought up a gentleman who wished to be introduced to her. He made himself extremely agreeable, but was a little too effusive with his complimentary speeches, telling her how delighted he was to meet her, and how much he had been wishing for that honour.

After hearing this two or three times she turned on him and asked him in the directest way why he had wished to see her so very much; then, anticipating that the answer would be that it was because of what he had heard of her charm, her linguistic, musical and various other accomplishments, and so on, she made ready to administer a nice little snub, when he made this very unexpected reply:

"O madame, how can you ask? You must know we all admire you because you are the only person in all Paris who has the courage and originality to decorate her *salon* with a human skull."

XXVII

A STORY OF A WALNUT

He was a small old man, curious to look at, and every day when I came out of my cottage and passed his garden he was there, his crutches under his arms, leaning on the gate, silently regarding me as I went by. Not boldly; his round dark eyes were like those of some shy animal peering inquisitively but shyly at the passer-by. His was a tumble-down old thatched cottage, leaky and miserable to live in, with about three-quarters of an acre of mixed garden and orchard surrounding it. The trees were of several kinds—cherry, apple, pear, plum, and one big walnut; and there were also shade trees, some shrubs and currant and gooseberry bushes, mixed with vegetables, herbs, and garden flowers. The man himself was in harmony with his disorderly but picturesque surroundings, his clothes dirty and almost in rags; an old jersey in place of a shirt, and over it two and sometimes three waistcoats of different shapes and sizes, all of one indeterminate earthy colour; and over these an ancient coat too big for the wearer. The thin hair, worn on the shoulders, was dust-colour mixed with grey, and to crown all there was a rusty rimless hat, shaped like an inverted flowerpot. From beneath this strange hat the small strange face, with the round, furtive, troubled eyes, watched me as I passed.

The people I lodged with told me his history. He had lived there many years, and everybody knew him, but nobody liked him,—a cunning, foxy, grabbing old rascal; unsocial, suspicious, unutterably mean. Never in all the years of his life in the village had he given a sixpence or a penny to anyone; nor a cabbage, nor an apple, nor had he ever lent a helping hand to a neighbour nor shown any neighbourly feeling.

He had lived for himself alone; and was alone in the world, in his miserable cottage, and no person had any pity for him in his loneliness and suffering now when he was almost disabled by rheumatism.

He was not a native of the village; he had come to it a young man, and some kindly-disposed person had allowed him to build a small hut as a shelter at the side of his hedge. Now the village was at one end of a straggling common, and many irregular strips and patches of common-land existed scattered about among the cottages and orchards. It was at a hedge-side on the border of one of these isolated patches that the young stranger, known as an inoffensive, diligent, and exceedingly quiet young man, set up his hovel. To protect it from the cattle he made a small ditch before it. This ditch he made very deep, and the earth thrown out he built into a kind of rampart, and by its outer edge he put a row of young holly plants, which a good-natured woodman made him a present of. He was advised to plant the holly behind the ditch, but he thought his plan the best, and to protect the young plants he made a little fence of odd sticks and bits of old wire and hoop iron. But the sheep would get in, so he made a new ditch; and then something else, until in the course of years the three-quarters of an acre had been appropriated. That was the whole history, and the pilfering had gone no further only because someone in authority had discovered and put a stop to it. Still, one could see that (in spite of the powers) a strip a few inches in breadth was being added annually to the estate.

I was so much interested in all this that from time to time I began to pause beside his gate to converse with him. By degrees the timid, suspicious expression wore away, and his eyes looked only wistful, and he spoke of his aches and pains as if it did him good to tell them to another.

I then left the village, but visited it from time to time, usually at intervals of some months, always to find him by his gate, on his own property, which he won for himself in the middle of the village, and from which he watched his neighbours moving about their cottages, going and coming, and was not of them. Then a whole year went by, and when I found him at the old gate in the old attitude, with the old wistful look in the eyes, he seemed glad to see me, and we talked of many things. We talked, that is, of the weather, with reference to the crops, and his rheumatism. What else in the world was there to talk of? He read no paper and heard no news and was of no politics; and if it can be said that he had a philosophy of life it was a low-down one, about on a level with that of a solitary old dog-badger who lives in an earth he has excavated for himself with infinite pains in a strong stubborn soil—his home and refuge in a hostile world.

Finally, casting about in my mind for some new subject of conversation—for I was reluctant to leave him soon after so long an absence—it occurred to me that we had not said anything about his one walnut tree. Of all the other trees and the fruit he had gathered from them he had already spoken. "By-the-way," I said, "did your walnut tree yield well this year?"

"Yes, very well," he returned; then he checked himself and said, "Pretty well, but I did not get much for them." And after a little hesitation he added, "That reminds me of something I had forgotten. Something I have been keeping for you—a little present."

He began to feel in the capacious pockets of his big outside waistcoat, but found nothing. "I must give it up," he said; "I must have mislaid it."

He seemed a little relieved, and at the same time a little disappointed; and by-and-by, on my remarking that he had not felt in all his pockets, began searching again, and in the end produced the lost something—a walnut! Holding it up a moment, he presented it to me with a little forward jerk of the hand and a little inclination of the head; and that little gesture, so unexpected in him, served to show that he had thought a good deal about giving the walnut away, and had looked on it as rather an important present. It was, perhaps, the only one he had ever made in his life. While giving it to me he said very nicely, "Pray make use of it."

The use I have made of it is to put it carefully away among other treasured objects, picked up at odd times in out-of-the-way places. It may be that some minute mysterious insect or infinitesimal mite—there is almost certain to be a special walnut mite—has found an entrance into this prized nut and fed on its oily meat, reducing it within to a rust-coloured powder. The grub or mite, or whatever it is, may do so at its pleasure, and flourish and grow fat, and rear a numerous family, and get them out if it can; but all these corroding processes and changes going on inside the shell do not in the least diminish my nut's intrinsic value.

XXVII

A STORY OF A JACKDAW

At one end of the Wiltshire village where I was staying there was a group of half-a-dozen cottages surrounded by gardens and shade trees, and every time I passed this spot on my way to and from the downs on that side, I was hailed by a loud challenging cry—a sort of "Hullo, who goes there!" Unmistakably the voice of a jackdaw, a pet bird no doubt, friendly and impudent as one always expects Jackie to be. And as I always like to learn the history of every pet daw I come across, I went down to the cottage the cry usually came from to make enquiries. The door was opened to me by a tall, colourless, depressed-looking woman, who said in reply to my question that she didn't own no jackdaw. There was such a bird there, but it was her husband's and she didn't know nothing about it. I couldn't see it because it had flown away somewhere and wouldn't be back for a long time. I could ask her husband about it; he was the village sweep, and also had a carpenter's shop.

I did not venture to cross-question her; but the history of the daw came to me soon enough—on the evening of the same day in fact. I was staying at the inn and had already become aware that the bar-parlour was the customary meeting-place of a majority of the men in that small isolated centre of humanity. There was no club nor institute or reading-room, nor squire or other predominant person to regulate things differently. The landlord, wise in his generation, provided newspapers liberally as well as beer, and had his reward.

The people who gathered there of an evening included two or three farmers, a couple of professional gentlemen—not the vicar; a man of property, the postman, the carrier, the butcher, the baker and other tradesmen, the farm and other labourers, and last, but not least, the village sweep. A curious democratic assembly to be met with in a rural village in a purely agricultural district, extremely conservative in politics.

I had already made the acquaintance of some of the people, high and low, and on that evening, hearing much hilarious talk in the parlour, I went in to join the company, and found fifteen or twenty persons present. The conversation, when I found a seat, had subsided into a quiet tone, but presently the door opened and a short, robust-looking man with a round, florid, smiling face looked in upon us.

"Hullo, Jimmy, what makes you so late?" said someone in the room. "We're waiting to hear the finish of all that trouble about your bird at home. Stolen any more of your wife's jewellery? Come in, and let's hear all about it."

"Oh, give him time," said another. "Can't you see his brain's busy inventing something new to tell us!"

"Inventing, you say!" exclaimed Jimmy, with affected anger. "There's no need to do that! That there bird does tricks nobody would think of."

Here the person sitting next to me, speaking low, informed me that this was Jimmy Jacob, the sweep, that he owned a pet jackdaw, known to every one in the village, and supposed to be the cleverest bird that ever was. He added that Jimmy could be very amusing about his bird.

"I'd already begun to feel curious about that bird of yours," I said, addressing the sweep. "I'd like very much to hear his history. Did you take him from the nest?"

"Yes, Jim," said the man next to me. "Tell us how you came by the bird; it's sure to be a good story."

Jimmy, having found a seat and had a mug of beer put before him, began by remarking that he knew someone had been interesting himself in that bird of his. "When I went home to tea this afternoon," he continued, "my missus, she says to me: 'There's that bird of yours again,' she says."

"'What bird,' says I. 'If you mean Jac,' says I, 'what's he done now?—out with it.'

"'We'll talk about what he's done bimeby,' says she. 'What I mean is, a gentleman called to ask about that bird.'

"'Oh, did he?' says I. 'Yes,' she says. 'I told him I didn't know nothing about it.

He could go and ask you. You'd be sure to tell him a lot.'

"'And what did the gentleman say to that?' says I.

"'He arsked me who you was, an' I said you was the sweep an' you had a carpenter's shop near the pub, and was supposed to do carpentering.'

"*Supposed* to do carpentering! That's how she said it.

"'And what did the gentleman say to that?' says I.

"'He said he thought he seen you at the inn, and I said that's just where he would see you.'

"'Anything more between you and the gentleman?' says I, and she said: 'No, nothing more except that he said he'd look you up and arst if you was a funny little fat man, sort of round, with a little red face.' And I said, 'Yes, that's him.'"

Here I thought it time to break in. "It's true," I said, "I called at your cottage and saw your wife, but there's no truth in the account you've given of the conversation I had with her."

There was a general laugh. "Oh, very well," said Jimmy. "After that I've nothing more to say about the bird or anything else."

I replied that I was sorry, but we need not begin our acquaintance by quarrelling—that it would be better to have a drink together.

Jimmy smiled consent, and I called for another pint for Jimmy and a soda for myself; then added I was so sorry he had taken it that way as I should have liked to hear how he got his bird.

He answered that if I put it that way he wouldn't mind telling me. And everybody was pleased, and composed ourselves once more to listen.

"How I got that there bird was like this," he began. "It were about half after four in the morning, summer before last, an' I was just having what I may call my beauty sleep, when all of a sudden there came a most thundering rat-a-tat-tat at the door.

"'Good Lord,' says my missus, 'whatever is that?'

"'Sounds like a knock at the door,' says I. 'Just slip on your thingamy an' go see.'

"'No,' she says, 'you must go, it might be a man.'

"'No,' I says, 'it ain't nothing of such consekince as that. It's only an old woman come to borrow some castor oil.'

"So she went and bimeby comes back and says: 'It's a man that's called to see you an' it's very important.'

"'Tell him I'm in bed,' says I, 'and can't get up till six o'clock.'

"Well, after a lot of grumbling, she went again, then came back and says the man won't go away till he seen me, as it's very important. 'Something about a bird,' she says.

"'A bird!' I says, 'what d'you mean by a bird?'

"'A rook!' she says.

"'A rook!' says I. 'Is he a madman, or what?'

"'He's a man at the door,' she says, 'an' he won't go away till he sees you, so you'd better git up and see him.'

"'All right, old woman,' I says, 'I'll git up as you say I must, and I'll smash him. Get me something to put on,' I says.

"'No,' she says, 'don't smash him'; and she give me something to put on, weskit and trousers, so I put on the weskit and got one foot in a slipper, and went out to him with the trousers in my hand. And there he was at the door, sure enough, a tramp!

"'Now, my man,' says I, very severe-like, 'what's this something important you've got me out of bed at four of the morning for? Is it the end of the world, or what?'

"He looked at me quite calm and said it was something important but not that—not the end of the world. 'I'm sorry to disturb you,' he says, 'but women don't understand things properly,' he says, 'an' I always think it best to speak to a man.'

"'That's all very well,' I says, 'but how long do you intend to keep me here with nothing but this on?'

"'I'm just coming to it,' he says, not a bit put out. 'It's like this,' he says. 'I'm from the north—Newcastle way—an' on my way to Dorchester, looking for work,' he says.

"'Yes, I see you are!' says I, looking him up and down, fierce-like.

"'Last evening,' he says, 'I come to a wood about a mile from this 'ere village, and I says to myself, "I'll stay here and go on in the morning." So I began looking about and found some fern and cut an armful and made a bed under a oak-tree. I slep' there till about three this morning. When I opened my eyes, what should I see but a bird sitting on the ground close to me? I no sooner see it than I says to myself, "That bird is as good as a breakfast," I says. So I just put out my hand and copped it. And here it is!' And out he pulled a bird from under his coat.

"'That's a young jackdaw,' I says.

"'You may call it a jackdaw if you like,' says he; 'but what I want you to understand is that it ain't no ornary bird. It's a bird,' he says, 'that'll do you hansom and you'll be proud to have, and I've called here to make you a present of it. All I want is a bit of bread, a pinch of tea, and some sugar to make my breakfast in an hour's time when I git to some cottage by the road where they got a fire lighted,' he says.

"When he said that, I burst out laughing, a foolish thing to do, mark you, for when you laugh, you're done for; but I couldn't help it for the life of me. I'd seen many tramps but never such a cool one as this.

"I no sooner laughed than he put the bird in my hands, and I had to take it. 'Good Lord!' says I. Then I called to the missus to fetch me the loaf and a knife, and when I got it I cut him off half the loaf. 'Don't give him that,' she says: I'll cut him a piece.' But all I says was, 'Go and git me the tea.'

"'There's a very little for breakfast,' she says. But I made her fetch the caddy, and he put out his hand and I half filled it with tea. 'Isn't that enough?' says I; 'well, then, have some more,' I says; and he had some more. Then I made her fetch the bacon and began cutting him rashers. 'One's enough,' says the old woman. 'No,' says I, 'let him have a good breakfast. The bird's worth it,' says I and went on cutting him bacon. 'Anything more?' I arst him.

"'If you've a copper or two to spare,' he says, 'it'll be a help to me on my way to Dorchester.' "'Certainly,' says I, and I began to feel in my trouser pockets and found a florin. 'Here,' I says, 'it's all I have, but you're more than welcome to it.'

"Then my missus she giv' a sort of snort, and walked off.

"'And now,' says I, 'per'aps you won't mind letting me go back to git some clothes on.'

"In one minute,' he says, and went on calmly stowing the things away, and when he finished, he looks at me quite serious, and says, 'I'm obliged to you,' he says, 'and I hope you haven't ketched cold standing with your feet on them bricks and nothing much on you,' he says. 'But I want most particular to arst you not to forget to remember about that bird I giv' you,' he says. 'You call it a jackdaw, and I've no particular objection to that, only don't go and run away with the idea that it's just an or'nary jackdaw. It's a different sort, and you'll come to know its value bime-by, and that it ain't the kind of bird you can buy with a bit of bread and a pinch of tea,' he says. 'And there's something else you've got to think of—that wife of yours. I've been sort of married myself and can feel for you,' he says. 'The time will come when that there bird's pretty little ways will amuse her, and last of all it'll make her smile, and you'll get the benefit of that,' he says. 'And you'll remember the bird was giv' to you by a man named Jones—that's my name, Jones—walking from Newcastle to Dorchester, looking for work. A poor man, you'll say, down on his luck, but not one of the common sort, not a greedy, selfish man, but a man that's always trying to do something to make others happy,' he says.

"And after that, he said, 'Good-bye,' without a smile, and walked off.

"And there at the door I stood, I don't know how long, looking after him going down the road. Then I laughed; I don't know that I ever laughed so much in my life, and at last I had to sit down on the bricks to go on laughing more comfortably, until the missus came and arst me, sarcastic-like, if I'd got the high-strikes, and if she'd better get a bucket of water to throw over me.

"I says, 'No, I don't want no water. Just let me have my laugh out and then it'll be all right.' Well, I don't see nothing to laugh at,' she says. 'And I s'pose you thought you giv' him a penny. Well, it wasn't a penny, it was a florin,' she says.

"'And little enough, too,' I says. 'What that man said to me, to say nothing of the bird, was worth a sovereign. But you are a woman, and can't understand that,' I says. 'No,' she says, 'I can't, and lucky for you, or we'd 'a' been in the workhouse before now,' she says.

"And that's how I got the bird."

XXIX

A WONDERFUL STORY OF A MACKEREL

The angler is a mighty spinner of yarns, but no sooner does he set about the telling than I, knowing him of old, and accounting him not an uncommon but an unconscionable liar, begin (as Bacon hath it) "to droop and languish." Nor does the languishing end with the story if I am compelled to sit it out, for in that state I continue for some hours after. But oh! the difference when someone who is not an angler relates a fishing adventure! A plain truthful man who never dined at an anglers' club, nor knows that he who catches, or tries to catch a fish, must tell you something to astonish and fill you with envy and admiration. To a person of this description I am all attention, and however prosaic and even dull the narrative may be, it fills me with delight, and sends me happy to bed and (still chuckling) to a refreshing sleep.

Accordingly, when one of the "commercials" in the coffee-room of the Plymouth Hotel began to tell a wonderful story of a mackerel he once caught a very long time back, I immediately put down my pen so as to listen with all my ears. For he was about the last person one would have thought of associating with fish-catching—an exceedingly towny-looking person indeed, one who from his conversation appeared to know nothing outside of his business. He was past middle age—oldish-looking for a traveller—his iron-grey hair brushed well up to hide the baldness on top, disclosing a pair of large ears which stood out like handles; a hatchet face with parchment skin, antique side whiskers, and gold-rimmed glasses on his large beaky nose. He wore the whitest linen and blackest, glossiest broadcloth, a big black cravat, diamond stud in his shirt-front in the old fashion, and a heavy gold chain with a spade guinea attached. His get-up and general appearance, though ancient, or at all events mid-Victorian, proclaimed him a person of considerable importance in his vocation.

He had, he told us at starting, a very good customer at Bristol, perhaps the best he ever had, at any rate the one who had stuck longest to him, since what he was telling us happened about the year 1870. He went to Bristol expressly to see this man, expecting to get a good order from him, but when he arrived and saw the wife, and asked for her husband, she replied that he was away on his holiday with the two little boys. It was a great disappointment, for, of course, he couldn't get an order from her. Confound the woman! she was always against him; what she would have liked was to have half a dozen travellers dangling about her, so as to pit one against another and distribute the orders among them just as flirty females distribute their smiles, instead of putting trust in one.

Where had her husband gone for his holiday? he asked; she said Weymouth and then was sorry she had let it out. But she refused to give the address. "No, no," she said; "he's gone to enjoy himself, and mustn't be reminded of business till he gets back."

However, he resolved to follow him to Weymouth on the chance of finding him there, and accordingly took the next train to that place. And, he added, it was lucky for him that he did so, for he very soon found him with his boys on the front, and, in spite of what she said, it was not with this man as it was with so many others who refuse to do business when away from the shop. On the contrary, at Weymouth he secured the best order this man had given him up to that time; and it was because he was away from his wife, who had always contrived to be present at their business meetings, and was very interfering, and made her husband too cautious in buying.

It was early in the day when this business was finished. "And now," said the man from Bristol, who was in a sort of gay holiday mood, "what are you going to do with yourself for the rest of the day?"

He answered that he was going to take the next train back to London. He had finished with Weymouth—there was no other customer there.

Here he digressed to tell us that he was a beginner at that time at the salary of a pound a week and fifteen shillings a day for travelling expenses. He thought this a great thing at first; when he heard what he was to get he walked about on air all day long, repeating to himself, "Fifteen shillings a day for expenses!" It was incredible; he had been poor, earning about five shillings a week, and now he had suddenly come into this splendid fortune. It wouldn't be much for him now! He began by spending recklessly; and in a short time discovered that the fifteen shillings didn't go far; now he had come to his senses and had to practise a rigid economy. Accordingly, he thought he would save the cost of a night's lodging and go back to town. But the Bristol man was anxious to keep him and said he had hired a man and boat to go fishing with the boys,—why couldn't he just engage a bedroom for the night and spend the afternoon with them?

After some demur he consented, and took his bag to a modest Temperance Hotel, where he secured a room, and then, protesting he had never caught a fish or seen one caught in his life, he got into the boat, and was taken into the bay where he was to have his first and only experience of fishing. Perhaps it was no great thing, but it gave him something to remember all his life. After a while his line began to tremble and move about in an extraordinary way with sudden little tugs which were quite startling, and on pulling it in he found he had a mackerel on his hook. He managed to get it into the boat all right and was delighted at his good luck, and still more at the sight of the fish, shining like silver and showing the most beautiful colours. He had never seen anything so beautiful in his life! Later, the same thing happened again with the line and a second mackerel was caught, and altogether he caught three. His friend also caught a few, and after a most pleasant and exciting afternoon they returned to the town well pleased with their sport. His friend wanted him to take a share of the catch, and after a little persuasion he consented to take one, and he selected the one he had caught first, just because it was the first fish he had ever caught in his life, and it had looked more beautiful than any other, so would probably taste better.

Going back to the hotel he called the maid and told her he had brought in a mackerel which he had caught for his tea, and ordered her to have it prepared. He had it boiled and enjoyed it very much, but on the following morning when the bill was brought to him he found that he had been charged two shillings for fish.

"Why, what does this item mean?" he exclaimed. "I've had no fish in this hotel except a mackerel which I caught myself and brought back for my tea, and now I'm asked to pay two shillings for it? Just take the bill back to your mistress and tell her the fish was mine—I caught it myself in the Bay yesterday afternoon."

The girl took it up, and by-and-by returned and said her mistress had consented to take threepence off the bill as he had provided the fish himself.

"No," he said, indignantly, "I'll have nothing off the bill, I'll pay the full amount," and pay it he did in his anger, then went off to say goodbye to his friend, to whom he related the case.

His friend, being in the same hilarious humour as on the previous day, burst out laughing and made a good deal of fun over the matter.

That, he said, was the whole story of how he went fishing and caught a mackerel, and what came of it. But it was not quite all, for he went on to tell us that he still visited Bristol regularly to receive big and ever bigger orders from that same old customer of his, whose business had gone on increasing ever since; and invariably after finishing their business his friend remarks in a casual sort of way: "By the way, old man, do you remember that mackerel you caught at Weymouth which you had for tea, and were charged two shillings for?" "Then he laughs just as heartily as if it had only happened yesterday, and I leave him in a good humour, and say to myself: 'Now, I'll hear no more about that blessed mackerel till I go round to Bristol again in three months' time.'"

"How long ago did you say it was since you caught the mackerel?" I inquired.

"About forty years."

"Then," I said, "it was a very lucky fish for you—worth more perhaps than if a big diamond had been found in its belly. The man had got his joke—the one joke of his life perhaps—and was determined to stick to it, and that kept him faithful to you in spite of his wife's wish to distribute their orders among a lot of travellers."

He replied that I was perhaps right and that it had turned out a lucky fish for him. But his old customer, though his business was big, was not so important to him now when he had big customers in most of the large towns in England, and he thought it rather ridiculous to keep up that joke so many years.

XXX

STRANGERS YET

The man who composed that familiar delightful rhyme about blue eyes and black, and how you are to beware of the hidden knife in the one case and of a different sort of danger which may threaten you in the other, must have lived a good long time ago, or else be a very old man. Oh, so old, thousands of years, thousands of years, if all were told. And he, when he exhibited such impartiality, must have had other-coloured eyes himself. Most probably the sheep and goat eye, one which no person in his senses—except an anthropologist—can classify as either dark or light. It is that marmalade yellow, excessively rare in this country, but not very uncommon in persons of Spanish race. For who at this day, this age, after the mixing together of the hostile races has been going on these twenty centuries or longer, can believe that any inherited or instinctive animosity can still survive? If we do find such a feeling here and there, would it not be more reasonable to regard it as an individual antipathy, or as a prejudice, imbibed early in life from parents or others, which endures in spite of reason, long after its origin had been forgotten?

Nevertheless, one does meet with cases from time to time which do throw a slight shadow of doubt on the mind, and of several I have met I will here relate one.

At an hotel on the South Coast I met a Miss Browne, which is not her name, and I rather hope this sketch will not be read by anyone nearly related to her, as they might identify her from the description. A middle-aged lady with a brown skin, black hair and dark eyes, an oval face, fairly good-looking, her manner lively and attractive, her movements quick without being abrupt or jerky. She was highly intelligent and a good talker, with more to say than most women, and better able than most to express herself. We were at the same small table and got on well together, as I am a good listener and she knew—being a woman, how should she not?—that she interested me. One day at our table the conversation happened to be about the races of men and the persistence of racial characteristics, physical and mental, in persons of mixed descent. The subject interested her. "What would you call me?" she asked.

"An Iberian," I returned.

She laughed and said: "This makes the third time I have been called an Iberian, so perhaps it is true, and I'm curious to know what an Iberian is, and why I'm called an Iberian. Is it because I have something of a Spanish look?"

I answered that the Iberians were the ancient Britons, a dark-eyed, brown-skinned people who inhabited this country and all Southern Europe before the invasion of the blue-eyed races; that doubtless there had been an Iberian mixture in her ancestors, perhaps many centuries ago, and that these peculiar characters had come out strongly in her; she had the peculiar kind of blood in her veins and the peculiar sort of soul which goes with the blood.

"But what a mystery it is!" she exclaimed. "I am the only small one in a family of tall sisters. My parents were both tall and light, and the others took after them. I was small and dark, and they were tall blondes with blue eyes and pale gold hair. And in disposition I was unlike them as in physique. How do you account for it?"

It was a long question, I said, and I had told her all I could about it. I couldn't go further into it; I was too ignorant. I had just touched on the subject in one of my books. It was in other books, with reference to a supposed antagonism which still survives in blue-eyed and dark-eyed people.

She asked me to give her the titles of the books I spoke of. "You imagine, I daresay," she said, "that it is mere idle curiosity on my part. It isn't so. The subject has a deep and painful interest for me."

That was all, and I had forgotten all about the conversation until some time afterwards, when I had a letter from her recalling it. I quote one passage without the alteration of a syllable:

"Oh, why did I not know before, when I was young, in the days when my beautiful blue-eyed but cruel and remorseless mother and sisters made my life an inexplicable grief and torment! It might have lifted the black shadows from my youth by explaining the reason of their persecutions—it might have taken the edge from my sufferings by showing that I was not personally to blame, also that nothing could ever obviate it, that I but wasted my life and broke my heart in for ever vain efforts to appease an hereditary enemy and oppressor."

Cases of this kind cannot, however, appear conclusive. The cases in which mother and daughters unite in persecuting a member of the family are not uncommon. I have known several in my experience in which respectable, well-to-do, educated, religious people have displayed a perfectly fiendish animosity against one of the family. In all these cases it has been mother and daughters combining against one daughter, and so far as one can see into the matter, the cause is usually to be traced to some strangeness or marked peculiarity, physical or mental, in the persecuted one. The peculiarity may be a beauty of disposition, or some virtue or rare mental quality which the others do not possess.

It would perhaps be worth while to form a society to investigate all these cases of persecution in families, to discover whether or not they afford any support to the notion of an inherited antagonism of dark and light races. The Anthropological, Eugenic and Psychical Research Societies might consider the suggestion.

XXXI

THE RETURN OF THE CHIFF-CHAFF

(SPRING SADNESS)

On a warm, brilliant morning in late April I paid a visit to a shallow lakelet or pond five or six acres in extent which I had discovered some weeks before hidden in a depression in the land, among luxuriant furze, bramble, and blackthorn bushes. Between the thickets the boggy ground was everywhere covered with great tussocks of last year's dead and faded marsh grass—a wet, rough, lonely place where a lover of solitude need have no fear of being intruded on by a being of his own species, or even a wandering moorland donkey. On arriving at the pond I was surprised and delighted to find half the surface covered with a thick growth of bog-bean just coming into flower. The quaint three-lobed leaves, shaped like a grebe's foot, were still small, and the flowerstocks, thick as corn in a field, were crowned with pyramids of buds, cream and rosy-red like the opening dropwort clusters, and at the lower end of the spikes were the full-blown singular, snow-white, cottony flowers—our strange and beautiful water edelweiss.

A group of ancient, gnarled and twisted alder bushes, with trunks like trees, grew just on the margin of the pond, and by-and-by I found a comfortable arm-chair on the lower stout horizontal branches overhanging the water, and on that seat I rested for a long time, enjoying the sight of that rare unexpected loveliness.

The chiff-chaff, the common warbler of this moorland district, was now abundant, more so than anywhere else in England; two or three were flitting about among the alder leaves within a few feet of my head, and a dozen at least were singing within hearing, chiff-chaffing near and far, their notes sounding strangely loud at that still, sequestered spot. Listening to that insistent sound I was reminded of Warde Fowler's words about the sweet season which brings new life and hope to men, and how a seal and sanction is put on it by that same small bird's clear resonant voice. I endeavoured to recall the passage, saying to myself that in order to enter fully into the feeling expressed it is sometimes essential to know an author's exact words. Failing in this, I listened again to the bird, then let my eyes rest on the expanse of red and cream-coloured spikes before me, then on the masses of flame-yellow furze beyond, then on something else. I was endeavouring to keep my attention on these extraneous things, to shut my mind resolutely against a thought, intolerably sad, which had surprised me in that quiet solitary place. Surely, I said, this springtime verdure and bloom, this fragrance of the furze, the infinite blue of heaven, the bell-like double note of this my little feathered neighbour in the alder tree, flitting hither and thither, light and airy himself as a wind-fluttered alder leaf—surely this is enough to fill and to satisfy any heart, leaving no room for a grief so vain and barren, which nothing in nature suggested! That it should find me out here in this wilderness of all places—the place to which a man might come to divest himself of himself—that second self which he has unconsciously acquired—to be like the trees and animals, outside of the sad atmosphere of human life and its eternal tragedy! A vain effort and a vain thought, since that from which I sought to escape came from nature itself, from every visible thing; every leaf and flower and blade was eloquent of it, and the very sunshine, that gave life and brilliance to all things, was turned to darkness by it.

Overcome and powerless, I continued sitting there with half-closed eyes until those sad images of lost friends, which had risen with so strange a suddenness in my mind, appeared something more than mere memories and mentally-seen faces and forms, seen for a moment, then vanishing. They were with me, standing by me, almost as in life; and I looked from one to another, looking longest at the one who was the last to go; who was with me but yesterday, as it seemed, and stood still in our walk and turned to bid me listen to that same double note, that little spring melody which had returned to us; and who led me, waist-deep in the flowering meadow grasses to look for this same beautiful white flower which I had found here, and called it our "English edelweiss." How beautiful it all was! We thought and felt as one. That bond uniting us, unlike all other bonds, was unbreakable and everlasting. If one had said that life was uncertain it would have seemed a meaningless phrase. Spring's immortality was in us; ever-living earth was better than any home in the stars which eye hath not seen nor heart conceived. Nature was all in all; we worshipped her and her wordless messages in our hearts were sweeter than honey and the honeycomb.

To me, alone on that April day, alone on the earth as it seemed for a while, the sweet was indeed changed to bitter, and the loss of those who were one with me in feeling, appeared to my mind as a monstrous betrayal, a thing unnatural, almost incredible. Could I any longer love and worship this dreadful power that made us and filled our hearts with gladness—could I say of it, "Though it slay me yet will I trust it?"

By-and-by the tempest subsided, but the clouds returned after the rain, and I sat on in a deep melancholy, my mind in a state of suspense. Then little by little the old influence began to re-assert itself, and it was as if one was standing there by me, one who was always calm, who saw all things clearly, who regarded me with compassion and had come to reason with me. "Come now," it appeared to say, "open your eyes once more to the sunshine; let it enter freely and fill your heart, for there is healing in it and in all nature. It is true the power you have worshipped and trusted will destroy you, but you are living to-day and the day of your end will be determined by chance only. Until you are called to follow them into that 'world of light,' or it may be of darkness and oblivion, you are immortal. Think then of to-day, humbly putting away the rebellion and despondency corroding your life, and it will be with you as it has been; you shall know again the peace which passes understanding, the old ineffable happiness in the sights and sounds of earth. Common things shall seem rare and beautiful to you. Listen to the chiff-chaff ingeminating the familiar unchanging call and message of spring. Do you know that this frail feathered mite with its short, feeble wings has come back from an immense distance, crossing two continents, crossing mountains, deserts illimitable, and, worst of all, the salt, grey desert of the sea. North and north-east winds and snow and sleet assailed it when, weary with its long journey, it drew near to its bourne, and beat it back, weak and chilled to its little anxious heart, so that it could hardly keep itself from falling into the cold, salt waves. Yet no sooner is it here in the ancient home and cradle of its race, than, all perils and pains forgot, it begins to tell aloud the overflowing joy of the resurrection, calling earth to put on her living garment, to rejoice once more in the old undying gladness—that small trumpet will teach you something. Let your reason serve you as well as its lower faculties have served this brave little traveller from a distant land."

Is this then the best consolation my mysterious mentor can offer? How vain, how false it is!—how little can reason help us! The small bird exists only in the present; there is no past, nor future, nor knowledge of death. Its every action is the result of a stimulus from outside; its "bravery" is but that of a dead leaf or ball of thistle-down carried away by the blast. Is there no escape, then, from this intolerable sadness—from the thought of springs that have been, the beautiful multitudinous life that has vanished? Our maker and mother mocks at our efforts—at our philosophic refuges, and sweeps them away with a wave of emotion. And yet there is deliverance, the old way of escape which is ours, whether we want it or not. Nature herself in her own good time heals the wound she inflicts—even this most grievous in seeming when she takes away from us the faith and hope of reunion with our lost. They may be in a world of light, waiting our coming—we do not know; but in that place they are unimaginable, their state inconceivable. They were like us, beings of flesh and blood, or we should not have loved them. If we cannot grasp their hands their continued existence is nothing to us. Grief at their loss is just as great for those who have kept their faith as for those who have lost it; and on account of its very poignancy it cannot endure in either case. It fades, returning in its old intensity at ever longer intervals until it ceases. The poet of nature was wrong when he said that without his faith in the decay of his senses he would be worse than dead, echoing the apostle who said that if we had hope in this world only we should be of all men the most miserable. So, too, was the later poet wrong when he listened to the waves on Dover beach bringing the eternal notes of sadness in; when he saw in imagination the ebbing of the great sea of faith which had made the world so beautiful, in its withdrawal disclosing the deserts drear and naked shingles of the world. That desolation, as he imagined it, which made him so unutterably sad, was due to the erroneous idea that our earthly happiness comes to us from otherwhere, some region outside our planet, just as one of our modern philosophers has imagined that the principle of life on earth came originally from the stars.

The "naked shingles of the world" is but a mood of our transitional day; the world is just as beautiful as it ever was, and our dead as much to us as they have ever been, even when faith was at its highest. They are not wholly, irretrievably lost, even when we cease to remember them, when their images come no longer unbidden to our minds. They are present in nature: through ourselves, receiving but what we give, they have become part and parcel of it and give it an expression. As when the rain clouds disperse and the sun shines out once more, heaven and earth are filled with a chastened light, sweet to behold and very wonderful, so because of our lost ones, because of the old grief at their loss, the visible world is touched with a new light, a tenderness and grace and beauty not its own.

XXXII

A WASP AT TABLE

Even to a naturalist with a tolerant feeling for all living things, both great and small, it is not always an unmixed pleasure to have a wasp at table. I have occasionally felt a considerable degree of annoyance at the presence of a self-invited guest of that kind.

Some time ago when walking I sat down at noon on a fallen tree-trunk to eat my luncheon, which consisted of a hunk of cake and some bananas. The wind carried the fragrance of the fruit into the adjacent wood, and very soon wasps began to arrive, until there were fifteen or twenty about me. They were so aggressive and greedy, almost following every morsel I took into my mouth, that I determined to let them have as much as they wanted—*and something more*! I proceeded to make a mash of the ripest portions of the fruit mixed with whisky from my pocket-flask, and spread it nicely on the bark. At once they fell on it with splendid appetites, but to my surprise the alcohol produced no effect. I have seen big locusts and other important insects tumbling about and acting generally as if demented after a few sips of rum and sugar, but these wasps, when they had had their full of banana and whisky, buzzed about and came and went and quarrelled with one another just as usual, and when I parted from them there was not one of the company who could be said to be the worse for liquor. Probably there is no more steady-headed insect than the wasp, unless it be his noble cousin and prince, the hornet, who has a quite humanlike unquenchable thirst for beer and cider.

But the particular wasp at table I had in my mind remains to be spoken of. I was lunching at the house of a friend, the vicar of a lonely parish in Hampshire, and besides ourselves there were five ladies, four of them young, at our round table. The window stood open, and by-and-by a wasp flew in and began to investigate the dishes, the plates, then the eaters themselves, impartially buzzing before each face in turn. On his last round, before taking his departure, he continued to buzz so long before my face, first in front of one eye then the other, as if to make sure that they were fellows and had the same expression, that I at length impatiently remarked that I did not care for his too flattering attentions. And that was really the only inconsiderate or inhospitable word his visit had called forth. Yet there were, I have said, five ladies present! They had neither welcomed nor repelled him, and had not regarded him; and although it was impossible to be unconscious of his presence at table, it was as if he had not been there. But then these ladies were cyclists: one, in addition to the beautiful brown colour with which the sun had painted her face, showed some dark and purple stains on cheek and forehead—marks of a resent dangerous collision with a stone wall at the foot of a steep hill.

Here I had intended telling about other meetings with other wasps, but having touched on a subject concerning which nothing is ever said and volumes might be written—namely, the Part played by the bicycle in the emancipation of women—I will go on with it. That they are not really emancipated doesn't matter, since they move towards that goal, and doubtless they would have gone on at the same old, almost imperceptible rate for long years but for the sudden impulse imparted by the wheel. Middle-aged people can recall how all England held up its hands and shouted "No, no!" from shore to shore at the amazing and upsetting spectacle of a female sitting astride on a safety machine, indecently moving her legs up and down just like a man. But having tasted the delights of swift easy motion, imparted not by any extraneous agency, but—oh, sweet surprise!—by her own in-dwelling physical energy, she refused to get off. By staying on she declared her independence; and we who were looking on—some of us—rejoiced to see it; for did we not also see, when these venturesome leaders returned to us from careering unattended over the country, when easy motion had tempted them long distances into strange, lonely places, where there was no lover nor brother nor any chivalrous person to guard and rescue them from innumerable perils—from water and fire, mad bulls and ferocious dogs, and evil-minded tramps and drunken, dissolute men, and from all venomous, stinging, creeping, nasty, horrid things—did we not see that they were no longer the same beings we had previously known, that in their long flights in heat and cold and rain and wind and dust they had shaken off some ancient weakness that was theirs, that without loss of femininity they had become more like ourselves in the sense that they were more self-centred and less irrational?

But women, alas! can seldom follow up a victory. They are, as even the poet when most anxious to make the best of them mournfully confesses:

variable as the shade
By the light quivering aspen made.

Inconstant in everything, they soon cast aside the toy which had taught them so great a lesson and served them so well, carrying them so far in the direction they wished to go. And no sooner had they cast it aside than a fresh toy, another piece of mechanism, came on the scene to captivate their hearts, and instead of a help, to form a hindrance. The motor not only carried them back over all the ground they had covered on the bicycle, but further still, almost back to the times of chairs and fans and smelling-salts and sprained ankles at Lyme Regis. A painful sight was the fair lady not yet forty and already fat, overclothed and muffled up in heavy fabrics and furs, a Pekinese clasped in her arms, reclining in her magnificent forty-horse-power car with a man (*Homo sapiens*) in livery to drive her from shop to shop and house to house. One could shut one's eyes until it passed—shut them a hundred or five hundred times a day in every thoroughfare in every town in England; but alas! one couldn't shut out the fact that this spectacle had fascinated and made captive the soul of womankind, that it was now their hope, their dream, their beautiful ideal—the one universal ideal that made all women sisters, from the greatest ladies in the land downwards, and still down, from class to class, even to the semi-starved ragged little pariah girl scrubbing the front steps of a house in Mean Street for a penny.

The splendid spectacle has now been removed from their sight, but is it out of mind? Are they not waiting and praying for the war to end so that there may be petrol to buy and men returned from the front to cast off their bloodstained clothes and wash and bleach their blackened faces, to put themselves in a pretty livery and drive the ladies and their Pekinese once more?

A friend of mine once wrote a charming booklet entitled *Wheel Magic*, which was all about his rambles on the machine and its effect on him. He is not an athlete—on the contrary he is a bookish man who has written books enough to fill a cart, and has had so much to do with books all his life that one might imagine he had by some strange accident been born in the reading-room of the British Museum; or that originally he had actually been a bookworm, a sort of mite, spontaneously engendered between the pages of a book, and that the supernatural being who presides over the reading-room had, as a little pleasantry, transformed him into a man so as to enable him to read the books on which he had previously nourished himself.

I can't follow my friend's wanderings and adventures as, springing out of his world of books, he flits and glides like a vagrant, swift-winged, irresponsible butterfly about the land, sipping the nectar from a thousand flowers and doing his hundred miles in a day and feeling all the better for it, for this was a man's book, and the wheel and its magic was never a necessity in man's life. But it has a magic of another kind for woman, and I wish that some woman of genius would arise and, inspired perhaps by the ghost of Benjamin Ward Richardson in his prophetic mood, tell of this magic to her sisters. Tell them, if they are above labour in the fields or at the wash-tub, that the wheel, without fatiguing, will give them the deep breath which will purify the blood, invigorate the heart, stiffen the backbone, harden the muscles; that the mind will follow and accommodate itself to these physical changes; finally, that the wheel will be of more account to them than all the platforms in the land, and clubs of all the pioneers and colleges, all congresses, titles, honours, votes, and all the books that have been or ever will be written.

XXXIII

WASPS AND MEN

I now find that I must go back to the subject of my last paper on the wasp in order to define my precise attitude towards that insect. Then, too, there was another wasp at table, not in itself a remarkably interesting incident, but I am anxious to relate it for the following reason.

If there is one sweetest thought, one most cherished memory in a man's mind, especially if he be a person of gentle pacific disposition, whose chief desire is to live in peace and amity with all men, it is the thought and recollection of a good fight in which he succeeded in demolishing his adversary. If his fights have been rare adventures and in most cases have gone against him, so much the more will he rejoice in that one victory.

It chanced that a wasp flew into the breakfast room of a country house in which I was a guest, when we were all—about fourteen in number, mostly ladies, young and middle-aged—seated at the table. The wasp went his rounds in the usual way, dropping into this or that plate or dish, feeling foods with his antennae or tasting with his tongue, but staying nowhere, and as he moved so did the ladies, starting back with little screams and exclamations of disgust and apprehension. For these ladies, it hardly need be said, were not cyclists. Then the son of the house, a young gentleman of twenty-two, a footballer and general athlete, got up, pushed back his chair and said: "Don't worry, I'll soon settle his hash."

Then I too rose from my seat, for I had made a vow not to allow a wasp to be killed unnecessarily in my presence.

"Leave it to me, please," I said, "and I'll put him out in a minute."

"No, sit down," he returned. "I have said I'm going to kill it."

"You shall not," I returned; and then the two of us, serviettes in hand, went for the wasp, who got frightened and flew all round the room, we after it. After some chasing he rose high and then made a dash at the window, but instead of making its escape at the lower open part, struck the glass.

"Now I've got him!" cried my sportsman in great glee; but he had not got him, for I closed with him, and we swayed about and put forth all our strength, and finally came down with a crash on a couch under the window. Then after some struggling I succeeded in getting on top, and with my right hand on his face and my knee on his body to keep him pressed down, I managed with my left hand to capture the wasp and put him out.

Then we got up—he with a scarlet face, furious at being baulked; but he was a true sportsman, and without one word went back to his seat at the table.

Undoubtedly it was a disgraceful scene in a room full of ladies, but he, not I, provoked it and was the ruffian, as I'm sure he will be ready to confess if he ever reads this.

But why all this fuss over a wasp's life, and in such circumstances, in a room full of nervous ladies, in a house where I was a guest? It was not that I care more for a wasp than for any other living creature—I don't love them in the St. Francis way; the wasp is not my little sister; but I hate to see any living creature unnecessarily, senselessly, done to death. There are other creatures I can see killed without a qualm—flies, for instance, especially houseflies and the big blue-bottle; these are, it was formerly believed, the progeny of Satan, and modern scientists are inclined to endorse that ancient notion. The wasp is a redoubtable fly-killer, and apart from his merits, he is a perfect and beautiful being, and there is no more sense in killing him than in destroying big game and a thousand beautiful wild creatures that are harmless to man. Yet this habit of killing a wasp is so common, ingrained as it were, as to be almost universal among us, and is found in the gentlest and humanest person, and even the most spiritual-minded men come to regard it as a sort of religious duty and exercise, as the incident I am going to relate will show.

I came to Salisbury one day to find it full of visitors, but I succeeded in getting a room in one of the small family hotels. I was told by the landlord that a congress was being held, got up by the Society for the pursuit or propagation of Holiness, and that delegates, mostly evangelical clergymen and ministers of the gospel of all denominations, with many lay brothers, had come in from all over the kingdom and were holding meetings every day and all day long at one of the large halls. The three bedrooms on the same floor with mine, he said, were all occupied by delegates who had travelled from the extreme north of England.

In the evening I met these three gentlemen and heard all about their society and congress and its aim and work from them.

Next morning at about half-past six I was roused from sleep by a tremendous commotion in the room adjoining mine: cries and shouts, hurried trampings over the floor, blows on walls and windows and the crash of overthrown furniture. However, before I could shake my sleep off and get up to find out the cause, there were shouts of laughter, a proof that no one had been killed or seriously injured, and I went to sleep again.

At breakfast we met once more, and I was asked if I had been much disturbed by the early morning noise and excitement. They proceeded to explain that a wasp had got into the room of their friend—indicating the elderly gentleman who had taken the head of the table; and as he was an invalid and afraid of being stung, he had shouted to them to come to his aid. They had tumbled out of bed and rushed in, and before beginning operations had made him cover his face and head with the bedclothes, after which they started hunting the wasp. But he was too clever for them. They threw things at him and struck at him with their garments, pillows, slippers, whatever came to hand, and still he escaped, and in rushing round in their excitement everything in the room except the bedstead was overthrown. At last the wasp, tired out or terrified dropped to the floor, and they were on him like a shot and smashed him with the slippers they had in their hands.

"And you call yourselves religious men!" I remarked when they had finished their story and looked at me expecting me to say something.

They stared astonished at me, then exchanged glances and burst out laughing, and laughed as if they had heard something too excruciatingly funny. The elderly clergyman who had been saved from the winged man-eating dragon that had invaded his room managed at last to recover his gravity, and his friends followed suit; they then all three silently looked at me again as if they expected to hear something more.

Not to disappoint them, I started telling them about the life and work of a famous nobleman, one of England's great pro-consuls, who for many years had ruled over various countries in distant regions of the earth, and many barbarous and semi-savage nations, by whom he was regarded, for his wisdom and justice and sympathy with the people he governed, almost as a god. This great man, who was now living in retirement at home, had just founded a Society for the Protection of Wasps, and had so far admitted two of his friends who were in sympathy with his objects to membership. As soon as I heard of the society I had sent in an application to be admitted, too, and felt it would be a proud day for me if the founder considered me worthy of being the fourth member.

Having concluded my remarks, the three religious gentlemen, who had listened attentively and seriously to my praises of the great pro-consul, once more exchanged glances and again burst out laughing, and continued laughing, rocking in their chairs with laughter, until they could laugh no more for exhaustion, and the elderly gentleman removed his spectacles to wipe the tears from his eyes.

Such extravagant mirth surprised me in that grey-haired man who was manifestly in very bad health, yet had travelled over three hundred miles from his remote Cumberland parish to give the benefit of his burning thoughts to his fellow-seekers after holiness congregated at Salisbury from all parts of the country.

The gust of merriment having blown its fill, ending quite naturally in "minute drops from off the eaves," I gravely wished them good-bye and left the room. They did not know, they never suspected that the amusement had been on both sides, and that despite their laughter it had been ten times greater on mine than on theirs.

I can't in conclusion resist the temptation to tell just one more wasp incident, although I fear it will hurt the tender-hearted and religious reader's susceptibilities more than any of those I have already told. But it will be told briefly, without digression and moralisings.

We have come to regard Nature as a sort of providence who is mindful of us and recompenses us according to what our lives are—whether we worship her and observe her ordinances or find our pleasure in breaking them and mocking her who will not be mocked. But it is sad for those who have the feeling of kinship for all living things, both great and small, from the whale and the elephant down even to the harvest mouse and beetle and humble earthworm, to know that killing—killing for sport or fun—is not forbidden in her decalogue. If the killing at home is not sufficient to satisfy a man, he can transport himself to the Dark Continent and revel in the slaughter of all the greatest and noblest forms of life on the globe. There is no crime and no punishment and no comfort to those who are looking on, except some on exceedingly rare occasion when we receive a thrill of joy at the lamentable tidings of the violent death of some noble young gentleman beloved of everybody and a big-game hunter, who was elephant-shooting, when one of the great brutes, stung to madness by his wounds, turned, even when dying, on his persecutor and trampled him to death.

In a small, pretty, out-of-the-world village in the West of England I made the acquaintance of the curate, a boyish young fellow not long from Oxford, who was devoted to sport and a great killer. He was not satisfied with cricket and football in their seasons and golf and lawn tennis—he would even descend to croquet when there was nothing else—and boxing and fencing, and angling in the neighbouring streams, but he had to shoot something every day as well. And it was noticed by the villagers that the shooting fury was always strongest on him on Mondays. They said it was a reaction; that after the restraint of Sunday with its three services, especially the last when he was permitted to pour out his wild curatical eloquence, the need of doing something violent and savage was most powerful; that he had, so to say, to wash out the Sunday taste with blood.

One August, on one of these Mondays, he was dodging along a hedge-side with his gun trying to get a shot at some bird, when he unfortunately thrust his foot into a populous wasps' nest, and the infuriated wasps issued in a cloud and inflicted many stings on his head and face and neck and hands, and on other parts of his anatomy where they could thrust their little needles through his clothes.

This mishap was the talk of the village. "Never mind," they said cheerfully—they were all very cheerful over it—"he's a good sports-man, and like all of that kind, hard as nails, and he'll soon be all right, making a joke of it."

The result "proved the rogues, they lied," that he was not hard as nails, but from that day onwards was a very poor creature indeed. The brass and steel wires in his system had degenerated into just those poor little soft grey threads which others have and are subject to many fantastical ailments. He fell into a nervous condition and started and blanched and was confused when suddenly hailed or spoken to even by some harmless old woman. He trembled at a shadow, and the very sight and sound of a wasp in the breakfast room when he was trying to eat a little toast and marmalade filled him, thrilled him, with fantastic terrors never felt before. And in vain to still the beating of his heart he would sit repeating: "It's only a wasp and nothing more." Then some of the parishioners who loved animals, for there are usually one or two like that in a village, began to say that it was a "judgment" on him, that old Mother Nature, angry at the persecutions of her feathered children by this young cleric who was supposed to be a messenger of mercy, had revenged herself on him in that way, using her little yellow insects as her ministers.

XXXIV

IN CHITTERNE CHURCHYARD

Chitterne is one of those small out-of-the-world villages in the south Wiltshire downs which attract one mainly because of their isolation and loneliness and their unchangeableness. Here, however, you discover that there has been an important change in comparatively recent years—some time during the first half of the last century. Chitterne, like most villages, possesses one church, a big building with a tall spire standing in its central part. Before it was built there were two churches and two Chitternes—two parishes with one village, each with its own proper church. These were situated at opposite ends of the one long street, and were small ancient buildings, each standing in its own churchyard. One of these disused burying-places, with a part of the old building still standing in it, is a peculiarly attractive spot, all the more so because of long years of neglect and of ivy, bramble, and weed and flower of many kinds that flourish in it, and have long obliterated the mounds and grown over the few tombs and headstones that still exist in the ground.

It was an excessively hot August afternoon when I last visited Chitterne, and, wishing to rest for an hour before proceeding on my way, I went to this old churchyard, naturally thinking that I should have it all to myself. But I found two persons there, both old women of the peasant class, meanly dressed; yet it was evident they had their good clothes on and were neat and clean, each with a basket on her arm, probably containing her luncheon. For they were only visitors and strangers there, and strangers to one another as they were to me— that, too, I could guess: also that they had come there with some object— perhaps to find some long unvisited grave, for they were walking about, crossing and recrossing each other's track, pausing from time to time to look round, then pulling the ivy aside from some old tomb and reading or trying to read the worn, moss-grown inscription. I began to watch their movements with growing interest, and could see that they, too, were very much interested in each other, although for a long time they did not exchange a word. Presently I, too, fell to examining the gravestones, just to get near them, and while pretending to be absorbed in the inscriptions I kept a sharp eye on their movements. They took no notice of me. I was nothing to them—merely one of another class, a foreigner, so to speak, a person cycling about the country who was just taking a ten minutes' peep at the place to gratify an idle curiosity. But who was *she*—that other old woman; and what did she want hunting about there in this old forsaken churchyard? was doubtless what each of those two was saying to herself. And by-and-by their curiosity got the better of them; then contrived to meet at one stone which they both appeared anxious to examine.

I had anticipated this, and no sooner were they together than I was down on my knees busily pulling the ivy aside from a stone three or four yards from theirs, absorbed in my business. They bade each other good day and said something about the hot weather, which led one to remark that she had found it very trying as she had left home early to walk to Salisbury to take the train to Codford, and from there she had walked again to Chitterne. Oddly enough, the other old woman had also been travelling all day, but from an opposite direction, over Somerset way, just to visit Chitterne. It seemed an astonishing thing to them when it came out that they had both been looking forward for years to this visit, and that it should have been made on the same day, and that they should have met there in that same forsaken little graveyard. It seemed stranger still when they came to tell why they had made this long-desired visit. They were both natives of the village, and had both left it early in life, one aged seven, the other ten; they had left much about the same time, and had never returned until now. And they were now here with the same object—just to find the graves, unmarked by a stone, where the mother of one of them, the grandparents of both, and other relatives they still remembered had been buried more than half a century ago. They were surprised and troubled at their failure to identify the very spots where the mounds used to be. "It do all look so different," said one, "an' the old stones be mostly gone." Finally, when they told their names and their fathers' names—farm-labourers both—they failed to remember each other, and could only suppose that they must have forgotten many things about their far-off childhood, although others were still as well remembered as the incidents of yesterday.

The old dames had become very friendly and confidential by this time. "I dare say," I said to myself, "that if I can manage to stay to the end I shall see them embrace and kiss at parting," and I also thought that their strange meeting in the old village churchyard would be a treasured memory for the rest of their lives. I feared they would suspect me of eavesdropping, and taking out my penknife, I began diligently scraping the dead black moss from the letters on the stone, after which I made pretence of copying the illegible inscription in my notebook. They, however, took no notice of me, and began telling each other what their lives had been since they left Chitterne. Both had married working men and had lost their husbands many years ago; one was sixty-nine, the other in her sixty-sixth year, and both were strong and well able to work, although they had had hard lives. Then in a tone of triumph, their faces lighting up with a kind of joy, they informed each other that they had never had to go to the parish for relief. Each was anxious to be first in telling how it had come about that she, the poor widow of a working man, had been so much happier in her old age than so many others. So eager were they to tell it that when one spoke the other would cut in long before she finished, and when they talked together it was not easy to keep the two narratives distinct. One was the mother of four daughters, all still unmarried, earning their own livings, one in a shop, another a sempstress, two in service in good houses, earning good wages. Never had woman been so blessed in her children! They would never see their mother go to the House! The other had but one, a son, and not many like him; no son ever thought more of his mother. He was at sea, but every nine to ten months he was back in Bristol, and then on to visit her, and never let a month pass without writing to her and sending money to pay her rent and keep a nice comfortable home for him.

They congratulated one another; then the mother of four said she always thanked God for giving her daughters, because they were women and could feel for a mother. The other replied that it was true, she had often seen it, the way daughters stuck to their mother—*until they married*. She was thankful to have a son; a man, she said, is a man and can go out in the world and do things, and if he is a good son he will never see his mother want.

The other was nettled at that speech. "Of course a man's a man," she returned, "but we all know what men are. They are all right till they pick up with a girl who wants all their wages; then everyone, mother and all, must be given up." But a daughter was a daughter always; she had four, she was happy to say.

This made matters worse. "Daughters always daughters!" came the quick rejoinder. "I never learned that before. What, my son take up with a girl and leave his old mother to starve or go to the workhouse! I never heard such a foolish thing said in my life!" And, being now quite angry, she looked round for her basket and shawl so as to get away as quickly as possible from that insulting woman; but the other, guessing her intention, was too quick for her and started at once to the gate, but after going four or five steps turned and delivered her last shot: "Say what you like about your son, and I don't doubt he's been good to you, and I only hope it'll always be the same; but what I say is, give me a daughter, and I know, ma'am, that if you had a daughter you'd be easier in your mind!"

Having spoken, she made for the gate, and the other, stung in some vital part by the last words, stood motionless, white with anger, staring after her, first in silence, but presently she began talking audibly to herself. "My son—my son pick up with a girl! My son leave his mother to go on the parish!"—but I stayed to hear no more; it made me laugh and—it was too sad.

XXXV

A HAUNTER OF CHURCHYARDS

I said a little while ago that when staying at a village I am apt to become a haunter of its churchyard; but I go not to it in the spirit of our well-beloved Mr. Pecksniff. He, it will be remembered, was accustomed to take an occasional turn among the tombs in the graveyard at Amesbury, or wherever it was, to read and commit to memory the pious and admonitory phrases he found on the stones, to be used later as a garnish to his beautiful, elevating talk. The attraction for me, which has little to do with inscriptions, was partly stated in the last sketch, and I may come to it again by-and-by.

Nevertheless, I cannot saunter or sit down among these memorials without paying some attention to the lettering on them, and always with greatest interest in those which time and weather and the corrosive lichen have made illegible. The old stones that are no longer visited, on which no fresh-gathered flower is ever laid, which mark the last resting-places of the men and women who were once the leading members of the little rustic community, and are now forgotten for ever, whose bones for a century past have been crumbling to dust. And the children's children, and remoter descendants of these dead, where are they? since one refuses to believe that they inhabit this land any longer. Under what suns, then, by what mountains and what mighty rivers, on what great green or sun-parched plains and in what roaring cities in far-off continents? They have forgotten; they have no memory nor tradition of these buried ones, nor perhaps even know the name of this village where they lived and died. Yet we believe that something from these same dead survives in them—something, too, of the place, the village, the soil, an inherited memory and emotion. At all events we know that, wheresoever they may be, that their soul is English still, that they will hearken to their mother's voice when she calls and come to her from the very ends of the earth.

As to the modern stones with inscriptions made so plain that you can read them at a distance of twenty yards, one cultivates the art of not seeing them, since if you look attentively at them and read the dull formal inscription, the disgust you will experience at their extreme ugliness will drive you from the spot, and so cause you to miss some delicate loveliness lurking there, like a violet "half hidden from the eye." But I need not go into this subject here, as I have had my say about it in a well-known book—Hampshire Days.

The stones I look at are of the seventeenth, eighteenth and first half of the nineteenth centuries, for even down to the fifties of last century something of the old tradition lingered on, and not all the stones were shaped and lettered in imitation of an auctioneer's advertisement posted on a barn door.

In reading the old inscriptions, often deciphered with difficulty after scraping away the moss and lichen, we occasionally discover one that has the charm of quaintness, or which touches our heart or sense of humour in such a way as to tempt us to copy it into a note-book.

In this way I have copied a fair number, and in glancing over my old note-books containing records of my rambles and observations, mostly natural history, I find these old epitaphs scattered through them. But I have never copied an inscription with the intention of using it. And this for the sufficient reason that epitaphs collected in a book do not interest me or anyone. They are in the wrong place in a book and cannot produce the same effect as when one finds and spells them out on a weathered stone or mural tablet out or inside a village church. It is the atmosphere—the place, the scene, the associations, which give it its only value and sometimes make it beautiful and precious. The stone itself, its ancient look, half-hidden in many cases by ivy, and clothed over in many-coloured moss and lichen and aerial algae, and the stonecutter's handiwork, his lettering, and the epitaphs he revelled in—all this is lost when you take the inscription away and print it. Take this one, for instance, as a specimen of a fairly good seventeenth-century epitaph, from Shrewton, a village on Salisbury Plain, not far from Stonehenge:

HERE IS MY HOPE TILL TRVMP SHALL SOVND AND CHRIST FOR MEE DOTH CALL THEN SHALL I RISE FROM DEATH TO LIFE NOE MORETO DYE AT ALL

R HERE LIES THE BODY OF ROBET WANESBROVGH THE SD E O ED OF Y NAME W DEPART THIS R E LIFE DEC Y 9TH AODNI 1675

It would not be very interesting to put this in a book:

Here is my hope till trump shall sound

> And Christ for me doth call,
> Then shall I rise from death to life
> No more to die at all.

But it was interesting to find it there, to examine the old lettering and think perhaps that if you had been standing at the elbow of the old lapidary, two and a half centuries ago, you might have given him a wrinkle in the economising of space and labour. In any case, to find it there in the dim, rich interior of that ancient village church, to view it in a religious or reverent mood, and then by-and-by in the dusty belfry to stumble on other far older memorials of the same family, and finally, coming out into the sunny churchyard, to come upon the same name once more in an inscription which tells you that he died in 1890, aged 88. And you think it a good record after nine generations, and that the men who lie under these wide skies on these open chalk downs do not degenerate.

I have copied these inscriptions for a purpose of my own, just as one plucks a leaf or a flower and drops it between the pages of a book he is reading to remind him on some future occasion, when by chance he finds it again on opening the book at some future time, of the scene, the place, the very mood of the moment.

Now, after all said, I am going to quote a few of my old gleanings from gravestones, not because they are good of their kind—my collection will look poor and meagre enough compared with those that others have made—but I have an object in doing it which will appear presently in the comments.

Always the best epitaphs to be found in books are those composed by versifiers for their own and the reading public's amusement, and always the best in the collection are the humorous ones.

The first collection I ever read was by the Spanish poet, Martinez de la Rosa, and although I was a boy then, I can still remember one:

> Aqui Fray Diego reposa,
> Jamas hiso otra cosa.

Which, translated literally, means:

> Here Friar James reposes:
> He never did anything else.

This does well enough on the printed page, but would shock the mind if seen on a gravestone, and perhaps the rarest of all epitaphs are the humorous ones. But one is pleased to meet with the unconsciously humorous; the little titillation, the smile, is a relief, and does not take away the sense of the tragedy of life and the mournful end.

A good specimen of the unconsciously humorous epitaph is on a stone in the churchyard at Maddington, a small village in the Wiltshire Downs, dated 1843:

> These few lines have been procured
> To tell the pains which he endured,
> He was crushed to death by the fall
> Of an old mould'ring, tottering wall.
> All ye young people that pass by
> Remember this and breathe a sigh,
> Lord, let him hear thy pard'ning voice
> And make his broken bones rejoice.

A better one, from the little village of Mylor, near Falmouth, has I fancy been often copied:

> His foot it slipped and he did fall,
> Help! help! he cried, and that was all.

And still a better one I found in the churchyard of St. Margaret's at Lynn, to John Holgate, aged 27, who died in 1712:

> He hath gained his port and is at ease,
> And hath escapt ye danger of ye seas,
> His glass is run his life is gone,
> Which to my thought never did no man no wronge.

That last line is remarkable, for although its ten slow words have apparently fallen by chance into that form and express nothing but a little negative praise of their subject, they say something more by implication. They conceal a mournful protest against the cruelty and injustice of his lot, and remind us of the old Italian folk-song, "O Barnaby, why did you die?" With plenty of wine in the house and salad in the garden, how wrong, how unreasonable of you to die! But even while blaming you in so many words, we know, O Barnaby, that the decision came not from you, and was an outrage, but dare not say so lest he himself should be listening, and in his anger at one word should take us away too before our time. It is unconsciously humorous, yet with the sense of tears in it.

But there is no sense of tears in the unconscious humour of the solemn or pompous epitaph composed by the village ignoramus.

A century ago the village idiot was almost always a member of the little rustic community, and was even useful to it in two distinct ways. He was "God's Fool," and compassion and sweet beneficent instinct, or soul growths, flourished the more for his presence; and secondly, he was a perpetual source of amusement, a sort of free cinema provided by Nature for the children's entertainment. I am not sure that his removal has not been a loss to the little rural centres of life.

Side by side with the village idiot there was the pompous person who could not only read a book, but could put whole sentences together and even make rhymes, and who on these grounds took an important part in the life of the community. He was not only adviser and letter-writer to his neighbours, but often composed inscriptions for their gravestones when they were dead. But in the best specimen of this kind which I have come upon, I feel pretty sure, from internal evidence, that the buried man had composed his own epitaph, and probably designed the form of the stone and its ornamentation. I found this stone in the churchyard of Minturne Magna, in Dorset. The stone was five feet high and four and a half broad—a large canvas, so to speak. On the upper half a Tree of Knowledge was depicted, with leaves and apples, the serpent wound about the trunk, with Adam and Eve standing on either side. Eve is extending her arm, with an apple in her open hand, to Adam, and he, foolish man, is putting out a hand to take it. Then follows the extraordinary inscription:

>   Here lyeth the Body
>   Of Richard Elambert,
>   Late of Holnust, who died
> June 6, in the year 1805, in the
>   100 year of his age.
> Neighbours make no stay,
> Return unto the Lord,
> Nor put it off from day to day,
> For Death's a debt ye all must pay.
> Ye knoweth not how soon,
> It may be the next moment,
> Night, morning or noon.
> I set this as a caution
> To my neighbours in rime,
> God give grace that you
> May all repent in time.
> For what God has decreed,
> We surely must obey,
> For when please God to send
> His death's dart into us so keen,
> O then we must go hence
> And be no more here seen.

ALSO

> Handy lyeth here
> Dianna Elambert,
> Which was my only daughter dear,
> Who died Jan. 10, 1776,
> In the 18th year of her age.

Poor Diana deserved a less casual word!

Enough of that kind. The next to follow is the quite plain, sensible, narrative inscription, with no pretension to fine diction, albeit in rhyme. Oddly enough the most perfect example I have found is in the churchyard at Kew, which seems too near to London:

> Here lyith the bodies of Robert and Ann
> Plaistow, late of Tyre, Edghill, in Warwickshire,
> Dyed August 23, 1728.
> At Tyre they were born and bred
> And in the same good lives they led,
> Until they come to married state,
> Which was to them most fortunate.
> Near sixty years of mortal life
> They were a happy man and wife,
> And being so by Nature tyed
> When one fell sick the other dyed,
> And both together laid in dust
> To await the rising of the just.
> They had six children born and bred,
> And five before them being dead,
> Their only then surviving son
> Hath caused this stone for to be done.

After this little masterpiece I will quote no other in this class.

After copying some scores of inscriptions, we find that there has always been a convention or fashion in such things, and that it has been constantly but gradually changing during the last three centuries. Very few of the seventeenth century, which are the best, are now decipherable, out of doors at all events. In an old graveyard you will perhaps find two or three among two or three hundred stones, yet you believe that two to three hundred years ago the small space was as thickly peopled with stones as now. The two or three or more that have not perished are of the very hardest kind of stone, and the old letters often show that they were cut with great difficulty. We also find that apart from the convention of the age or time, there were local conventions or fashions. In some parts of the South of England you find numbers of enormous stones five feet high and nearly as broad. This mode has long vanished. But you find a resemblance in the inscriptions as well. Thus, wherever the Methodists obtained a firm hold on the community, you find the spirit of ugliness appearing in the village churchyard from the middle of the eighteenth century onwards, when the old ornate and beautiful stones with figures of winged cherubs bearing torches, scattering flowers or blowing trumpets, were the usual decorations, giving place to the plain or ugly stone with its square ugly lettering and the dull monotonous form of the inscription. "To the memory of Mr. Buggins of this parish, who died on February 27th, 1801, aged 67." And then, to save trouble and expense, a verse from a hymn, or the simple statement that he is asleep in Jesus, or is awaiting the resurrection.

I am inclined to blame Methodism for these horrors simply because it is, as we know, the cult of ugliness, but there may have been another cause for the change; it was perhaps to some extent a reaction against the stilted, the pompous and silly epitaph which one finds most common in the first half of the eighteenth century.

Here is a perfect specimen which I found at St. Just, in Cornwall, to a
Martin Williams, 1771:

> Life's but a snare, a Labyrinth of Woe
> Which wretched Man is doomed to struggle through.
> To-day he's great, to-morrow he's undone,
> And thus with Hope and Fear he blunders on,
> Till some disease, or else perhaps old Age
> Calls us poor Mortals trembling from the Stage.

An amusing variant of one of the commoner forms of that time appears at Lelant, a Cornish village near St. Ives:

> What now you are so once was me,
> What now I am that you will be,
> Therefore prepare to follow me.

No less remarkable in grammar as in the identical or perfect rhyme in the first and third lines. The author or adapter could have escaped this by making the two first the expression of the person buried beneath, and the third the comment from the outsider, as follows:

Therefore prepare to follow *she,*

It was a woman, I must say.

This form of epitaph is quite common, and I need not give here more examples from my notes, but the better convention coming down from the preceding age goes on becoming more and more modified all through the eighteenth, and even to the middle of the nineteenth century.

The following from St. Erth, a Cornish village, is a most suitable inscription on the grave of an old woman who was a nurse in the same family from 1750 to 1814:

> Time rolls her ceaseless course; the race of yore
> That danced our infancy on their knee
> And told our wondering children Legends lore
> Of strange adventures haped by Land and Sea,
> How are they blotted from the things that be!

There are many beautiful stones and appropriate inscriptions during all that long period, in spite of the advent of Mr. Buggins and his ugliness, and the charm and pathos is often in a phrase, a single line, as in this from St. Keverne, 1710, a widow's epitaph on her husband:

Rest here awhile, thou dearest part of me.

But let us now get back another century at a jump, to the Jacobean and Caroline period. And for these one must look as a rule in interiors, seeing that, where exposed to the weather, the lettering, if not the whole stone, has perished. Perhaps the best specimen of the grave inscription, lofty but not pompous, of that age which I have met with is on a tablet in Ripon Cathedral to Hugh de Ripley, a locally important man who died in 1637:

> Others seek titles to their tombs
> Thy deeds to thy name prove new wombes
> And scutcheons to deck their Herse
> Which thou need'st not like teares and vers.
> If I should praise thy thriving witt
> Or thy weighed judgment serving it
> Thy even and thy like straight ends
> Thy pitie to God and to friends
> The last would still the greatest be
> And yet all jointly less than thee.
> Thou studiedst conscience more than fame
> Still to thy gathered selfe the same.
> Thy gold was not thy saint nor welth
> Purchased by rapine worse than stealth
> Nor did'st thou brooding on it sit
> Not doing good till death with it.
> This many may blush at when they see

> What thy deeds were what theirs should be.
> Thou'st gone before and I wait now
> T'expect my when and wait my how
> Which if my Jesus grant like thine
> Who wets my grave's no friend of mine.

Rather too long for my chapter, but I quote it for the sake of the last four lines, characteristic of that period, the age of conceits, of the love of fantasticalness, of Donne, Crashaw, Vaughan.

A jump from Ripon of 600 odd miles to the little village of Ludgvan, near Penzance, brings us to a tablet of nearly the same date, 1635, and an inscription conceived in the same style and spirit. It is interesting, on account of the name of Catherine Davy, an ancestress of the famous Sir Humphry, whose marble statue stands before the Penzance Market House facing Market Jew Street.

> Death shall not make her memory to rott
> Her virtues were too great to be forgott.
> Heaven hath her soul where it must still remain
> The world her worth to blazon forth her fame
> The poor relieved do honour and bless her name.
> Earth, Heaven, World, Poor, do her immortalize
> Who dying lives and living never dies.

Here is another of 1640:

> Here lyeth the body of my Husband deare
> Whom next to God I did most love and fear.
> Our loves were single: we never had but one
> And so I'll be although that thou art gone.

Which means that she has no intention of marrying again. Why have I set this inscription down? Solely to tell how I copied it. I saw it on a brass in the obscure interior of a small village church in Dorset, but placed too high up on the wall to be seen distinctly. By piling seven hassocks on top of one another I got high up enough to read the date and inscription, but before securing the name I had to get quickly down for fear of falling and breaking my neck. The hassocks had added five feet to my six.

The convention of that age appears again in the following inscription from a tablet in Aldermaston church, in that beautiful little Berkshire village, once the home of the Congreves:

> Like borne, like new borne, here like dead they lie,
> Four virgin sisters decked with pietie

> Beauty and other graces which commend
> And made them like blessed in the end.

Which means they were very much like each other, and were all as pure in heart as new-born babes, and that they all died unmarried.

Where the epitaph-maker of that time occasionally went wrong was in his efforts to get his fantasticalness in willy-nilly, or in a silly play upon words, as in the following example from the little village of Boyton on the Wylie river, on a man named Barnes, who died in 1638:

> Stay Passenger and view a stack of corne
> Reaped and laid up in the Almighty's Barne
> Or rather Barnes of Choyce and precious grayne
> Put in his garner there still to remaine.

But in the very next village—that of Stockton—I came on the best I have found of that time. It is, however, a little earlier in time, before fantasticalness came into fashion, and in spirit is of the nobler age. It is to Elizabeth Potecary, who died in 1590.

> Here she interred lies deprived of breath
> Whose light of virtue once on Earth did shyne
> Who life contemned ne feared ghostly death
> Whom worlde ne worldlye cares could cause repine
> Resolved to die with hope in Heaven placed
> Her Christ to see whom living she embraced
> In paynes most fervent still in zeal most strong
> In death delighting God to magnifye
> How long will thou forgett me Lord! this cry
> In greatest pangs was her sweet harmonye
> Forgett thee? No! he will not thee forgett
> In books of Lyfe thy name for aye is set.

And with Elizabeth Potecary, that dear lady dead these three centuries and longer, I must bring this particular Little Thing to an end.

XXXVI

THE DEAD AND THE LIVING

The last was indeed in essence a small thing, but was running to such a great length it had to be ended before my selected best inscriptions were used up, also before the true answer to the question: "Why, if inscriptions do not greatly interest me, do I haunt churchyards?" was given. Let me give it now: it will serve as a suitable conclusion to what has already been said on the subject in this and in a former book.

When we have sat too long in a close, hot, brilliantly-lighted, over-crowded room, a sense of unutterable relief is experienced on coming forth into the pure, fresh, cold night and filling our lungs with air uncontaminated with the poisonous gases discharged from other lungs. An analogous sense of immense relief, of escape from confinement and joyful liberation, is experienced mentally when after long weeks or months in London I repair to a rustic village. Yet, like the person who has in his excitement been inhaling poison into his system for long hours, I am not conscious of the restraint at the time. Not consciously conscious. The mind was too exclusively occupied with itself—its own mind affairs. The cage was only recognised as a cage, an unsuitable habitation, when I was out of it. An example, this, of the eternal disharmony between the busy mind and nature—or Mother Nature, let us say; the more the mind is concentrated on its own business the blinder we are to the signals of disapproval on her kindly countenance, the deafer to her warning whispers in our ear.

The sense of relief is chiefly due to the artificiality of the conditions of London or town life, and no doubt varies greatly in strength in town and country-bred persons; in me it is so strong that on first coming out to where there are woods and fields and hedges, I am almost moved to tears.

We have recently heard the story of the little East-end boy on his holiday in a quiet country spot, who exclaimed: "How full of sound the country is! Now in London we can't hear the sound because of the noises." And as with sound—the rural sounds that are familiar from of old and find an echo in us—so with everything: we do not hear nor see nor smell nor feel the earth, which he is, physically and mentally, in such per-period, the years that run to millions, that it has "entered the soul"; an environment with which he is physically and mentally, in such perfect harmony that it is like an extension of himself into the surrounding space. Sky and cloud and wind and rain, and rock and soil and water, and flocks and herds and all wild things, with trees and flowers—everywhere grass and everlasting verdure—it is all part of men, and is me, as I sometimes feel in a mystic mood, even as a religious man in a like mood feels that he is in a heavenly place and is a native there, one with it.

Another less obvious cause of my feeling is that the love of our kind cannot exist, or at all events not unmixed with contempt and various other unpleasant ingredients, in people who live and have their being amidst thousands and millions of their fellow-creatures herded together. The great thoroughfares in which we walk are peopled with an endless procession, an innumerable multitude; we hardly see and do not look at or notice them, knowing beforehand that we do not know and never will know them to our dying day; from long use we have almost ceased to regard them as fellow-beings.

I recall here a tradition of the Incas, which tells that in the beginning a benevolent god created men on the slopes of the Andes, and that after a time another god, who was at enmity with the first, spitefully transformed them into insects. Here we have a contrary effect—it is the insects which have been transformed; the millions of wood-ants, let us say, inhabiting an old and exceedingly populous nest have been transformed into men, but in form only; mentally they are still ants, all silently, everlastingly hurrying by, absorbed in their ant-business. You can almost smell the formic acid. Walking in the street, one of the swarming multitude, you are in but not of it. You are only one with the others in appearance; in mind you are as unlike them as a man is unlike an ant, and the love and sympathy you feel towards them is about equal to that which you experience when looking down on the swarm in a wood-ants' nest.

Undoubtedly when I am in the crowd, poisoned by contact with the crowd-mind—the formic acid of the spirits—I am not actually or keenly conscious of the great gulf between me and the others, but, as in the former case, the sense of relief is experienced here too in escaping from it. The people of the small rustic community have not been de-humanised. I am a stranger, and they do not meet me with blank faces and pass on in ant-like silence. So great is the revulsion that I look on them as of my kin, and am so delighted to be with them again after an absence of centuries, that I want to embrace and kiss them all. I am one of them, a villager with the village mind, and no wish for any other.

This mind or heart includes the dead as well as the living, and the church and churchyard is the central spot and half-way house or camping-ground between this and the other world, where dead and living meet and hold communion—a fact that is unknown to or ignored by persons of the "better class," the parish priest or vicar sometimes included.

And as I have for the nonce taken on the village mind, I am as much interested in my incorporeal, invisible neighbours as in those I see and am accustomed to meet and converse with every day. They are here in the churchyard, and I am pleased to be with them. Even when I sit, as I sometimes do of an evening, on a flat tomb with a group of laughing children round me, some not yet tired of play, climbing up to my side only to jump down again, I am not oblivious of their presence. They are there, and are glad to see the children playing among the tombs where they too had their games a century ago. I notice that the village woman passing through the ground pauses a minute with her eyes resting on a certain spot; even the tired labourer, coming home to his tea, will let his eyes dwell on some green mound, to see sitting or standing there someone who in life was very near and dear to him, with whom he is now exchanging greetings. But the old worn-out labourer, who happily has not gone to end his days in captivity in the bitter Home of the Poor—he, sitting on a tomb to rest and basking in the sunshine, has a whole crowd of the vanished villagers about him.

It is useless their telling us that when we die we are instantly judged and packed straight off to some region where we are destined to spend an eternity. We know better. Nature, our own hearts, have taught us differently. Furthermore, we have heard of the resurrection—that the dead will rise again at the last day; and with all our willingness to believe what our masters tell us, we know that even a dead man can't be in two places at the same time. Our dead are here where we laid them; sleeping, no doubt, but not so soundly sleeping, we imagine, as not to see and hear us when we visit and speak to them. And being villagers still though dead, they like to see us often, whenever we have a few spare minutes to call round and exchange a few words with them.

This extremely beautiful—and in its effect beneficial—feeling and belief, or instinct, or superstition if the superior inhabitants of the wood-ants' nest, who throw their dead away and think no more about them, will have it so—is a sweet and pleasant thing in the village life and a consolation to those who are lonely. Let me in conclusion give an instance.

The churchyard I like best is situated in the village itself, and is in use both for the dead and living, and the playground of the little ones, but some time ago I by chance discovered one which was over half a mile from the village; an ancient beautiful church and churchyard which so greatly attracted me that in my rambles in that part I often went a mile or two out of my way just for the pleasure of spending an hour or two in that quiet sacred spot. It was in a wooded district in Hampshire, and there were old oak woods all round the church, with no other building in sight and seldom a sound of human life. There was an old road outside the gate, but few used it. The tombs and stones were many and nearly covered with moss and lichen and half-draped in creeping ivy. There, sitting on a tomb, I would watch the small woodland birds that made it their haunt, and listen to the delicate little warbling or tinkling notes, and admire the two ancient picturesque yew trees growing there.

One day, while sitting on a tomb, I saw a woman coming from the village with a heavy basket on her head, and on coming to the gate she turned in, and setting the basket down walked to a spot about thirty yards from where I sat, and at that spot she remained for several minutes standing motionless, her eyes cast down, her arms hanging at her sides. A cottage woman in a faded cotton gown, of a common Hampshire type, flat-chested, a rather long oval face, almost colourless, and black dusty hair. She looked thirty-five, but was probably less than thirty, as women of their class age early in this county and get the toil-worn, tired face when still young.

By-and-by I went over to her and asked her if she was visiting some of her people at that spot. Yes, she returned; her mother and father were buried under the two grass mounds at her feet; and then quite cheerfully she went on to tell me all about them—how all their other children had gone away to live at a distance from home, and she was left alone with them when they grew old and infirm. They were natives of the village, and after they were both dead, five years ago, she got a place at a farm about a mile up the road. There she had been ever since, but fortunately she had to come to the village every week, and always on her way back she spent a quarter or half an hour with her parents. She was sure they looked for that weekly visit from her, as they had no other relation in the place now, and that they liked to hear all the village news from her.

All this and more she told me in the most open way. Like Wordsworth's "simple child," what could she know of death? But being a villager myself I was better informed than Wordsworth, and didn't enter on a ponderous argument to prove to her that when people die they die, and being dead, they can't be alive—therefore to pay them a weekly visit and tell them all the news was a mere waste of time and breath.

XXXVII

A STORY OF THREE POEMS

I wrote in the last sketch but one of the villager with a literary gift who composes the epitaphs in rhyme of his neighbours when they pass away and are buried in the churchyard. This has served to remind me of a kindred subject—the poetry or verse (my own included) of those who are not poets by profession: also of an incident. Undoubtedly there is a vast difference between the village rhymester and the true poet, and the poetry I am now concerned with may be said to come somewhat between these two extremes. Or to describe it in metaphor, it may be said to come midway between the crow of the "tame villatic fowl" and the music of the nightingale in the neighbouring copse or of the skylark singing at heaven's gate. The impartial reader may say at the finish that the incident was not worth relating. Are there any such readers? I doubt it. I take it that we all, even those who appear the most matter-of-fact in their minds and lives, have something of the root, the elements, of poetry in their composition. How should it be otherwise, seeing that we are all creatures of like passions, all in some degree dreamers of dreams; and as we all possess the faculty of memory we must at times experience emotions recollected in tranquillity. And that, our masters have told us, is poetry.

It is hardly necessary to say that it is nothing of the sort: it is the elements, the essence, the feeling which makes poetry if expressed. I have a passion for music, a perpetual desire to express myself in music, but as I can't sing and can't perform on any musical instrument, I can't call myself a musician. The poetic feeling that is in us and cannot be expressed remains a secret untold, a warmth in the heart, a rapture which cannot be communicated. But it cries to be told, and in some rare instances the desire overcomes the difficulty: in a happy moment the unknown language is captured as by a miracle and the secret comes out.

And, as a rule, when it has been expressed it is put in the fire, or locked up in a desk. By-and-by the hidden poem will be taken out and read with a blush. For how could he, a practical-minded man, with a wholesome contempt for the small scribblers and people weak in their intellectuals generally, have imagined himself a poet and produced this pitiful stuff!

Then, too, there are others who blush, but with pleasure, at the thought that, without being poets, they have written something out of their own heads which, to them at all events, reads just like poetry. Some of these little poems find their way into an editor's hands, to be looked at and thrown aside in most cases, but occasionally one wins a place in some periodical, and my story relates to one of these chosen products—or rather to three.

One summer afternoon, many years ago—but I know the exact date: July 1st, 1897—I was drinking tea on the lawn of a house at Kew, when the maid brought the letters out to her mistress, and she, Mrs. E. Hubbard, looking over the pile remarked that she saw the *Selborne Magazine* had come and she would just glance over it to see if it contained anything to interest both of us.

After a minute or two she exclaimed "Why, here is a poem by Charlie Longman! How strange—I never suspected him of being a poet!"

She was speaking of C. J. Longman, the publisher, and it must be explained that he was an intimate friend and connection of hers through his marriage with her niece, the daughter of Sir John Evans the antiquary, and sister of Sir Arthur Evans.

The poem was *To the Orange-tip Butterfly*.

Cardamines! Cardamines!
  Thine hour is when the thrushes sing,
When gently stirs the vernal breeze,
  When earth and sky proclaim the spring;
When all the fields melodious ring
  With cuckoos' calls, when all the trees
Put on their green, then art thou king
  Of butterflies, Cardamines.

What though thine hour be brief, for thee
  The storms of winter never blow,
No autumn gales shall scorn the lea,
  Thou scarce shalt feel the summer's glow;
But soaring high or flitting low,
Or racing with the awakening bees
For spring's first draughts of honey—so
  Thy life is passed, Cardamines.

Cardamines! Cardamines!
  E'en among mortal men I wot
Brief life while spring-time quickly flees
  Might seem a not ungrateful lot:
For summer's rays are scorching hot
  And autumn holds but summer's lees,
And swift in autumn is forgot
  The winter comes, Cardamines.

So well pleased were we with this little lyric that we read it aloud two or three times over to each other: for it was a hot summer's day when the early, freshness and bloom is over and the foliage takes on a deeper, almost sombre green; and it brought back to us the vivid spring feeling, the delight we had so often experienced on seeing again the orange-tip, that frail delicate flutterer, the loveliest, the most spiritual, of our butterflies.

Oddly enough, the very thing which, one supposes, would spoil a lyric about any natural object—the use of a scientific instead of a popular name, with the doubling and frequent repetition of it—appeared in this instance to add a novel distinction and beauty to the verses.

The end of our talk on the subject was a suggestion I made that it would be a nice act on her part to follow Longman's lead and write a little nature poem for the next number of the magazine. This she said she would do if I on my part would promise to follow her poem with one by me, and I said I would.

Accordingly her poem, which I transcribe, made its appearance in the next number.

MY MOOR

Purple with heather, and golden with gorse,
  Stretches the moorland for mile after mile;
Over it cloud-shadows float in their course,—
  Grave thoughts passing athwart a smile,—
Till the shimmering distance, grey and gold,
Drowns all in a glory manifold.

O the blue butterflies quivering there,
  Hovering, flickering, never at rest,
Quickened flecks of the upper air
  Brought down by seeing the earth so blest;
And the grasshoppers shrilling their quaint delight
At having been born in a world so bright!

Overhead circles the lapwing slow,
  Waving his black-tipped curves of wings,
Calling so clearly that I, as I go,
  Call back an answering "Peewit," that brings
The sweep of his circles so low as he flies
That I see his green plume, and the doubt in his eyes.

Harebell and crowfoot and bracken and ling
  Gladden my heart as it beats all aglow
In a brotherhood true with each living thing,
  From the crimson-tipped bee, and the chaffer slow,
And the small lithe lizard, with jewelled eye,
To the lark that has lost herself far in the sky.

Ay me, where am I? for here I sit
  With bricks all round me, bilious and brown;
And not a chance this summer to quit
  The bustle and roar and the cries of town,
Nor to cease to breathe this over-breathed air,
Heavy with toil and bitter with care.

Well,—face it and chase it, this vain regret;
  Which would I choose, to see my moor
With eyes such as many that I have met,

Which see and are blind, which all wealth leaves poor,
Or to sit, brick-prisoned, but free within,
Freeborn by a charter no gold can win?

When my turn came, the poem I wrote, which duly appeared, was, like my friend's *Moor*, a recollected emotion, a mental experience relived. Mine was in the New Forest; when walking there on day, the loveliness of that green leafy world, its silence and its melody and the divine sunlight, so wrought on me that for a few precious moments it produced a mystical state, that rare condition of beautiful illusions when the feet are off the ground, when, on some occasions, we appear to be one with nature, unbodied like the poet's bird, floating, diffused in it. There are also other occasions when this transfigured aspect of nature produces the idea that we are in communion with or in the presence of unearthly entities.

THE VISIONARY

I

It must be true, I've somtimes thought,
That beings from some realm afar
Oft wander in the void immense,
  Flying from star to star.

In silence through this various world,
They pass, to mortal eyes unseen,
And toiling men in towns know not
  That one with them has been.

But oft, when on the woodland falls
A sudden hush, and no bird sings;
When leaves, scarce fluttered by the wind,
  Speak low of sacred things,

My heart has told me I should know,
In such a lonely place, if one
From other worlds came there and stood
  Between me and the sun.

II

At noon, within the woodland shade
I walked and listened to the birds;

And feeling glad like them I sang
  A low song without words.

When all at once a radiance white,
Not from the sun, all round me came;
The dead leaves burned like gold, the grass
  Like tongues of emerald flame.

The murmured song died on my lips;
Scarce breathing, motionless I stood;
So strange that splendour was! so deep
  A silence held the wood!

The blood rushed to and from my heart,
Now felt like ice, now fire in me,
Till putting forth my hands, I cried,
  "O let me hear and see!"

But even as I spake, and gazed
Wide-eyed, and bowed my trembling knees,
The glory and the silence passed
  Like lightning from the trees.

And pale at first the sunlight seemed
When it was gone; the leaves were stirred
To whispered sound, and loud rang out
  The carol of a bird.

www.ingramcontent.com/pod-product-compliance
Lightning Source LLC
Chambersburg PA
CBHW081724100526
44591CB00016B/2491